T0115122

Advance Praise for
Crowned in Promise

"I'm so grateful to have a resource like *Crowned in Promise* to guide my prayers for my children. This book is a gift to parents everywhere who desperately want to approach God's throne of grace on behalf of our children. It is an honor to pray for our children! And if we don't pray for them, who will?"

—ESTHER FLEECE ALLEN, bestselling author of *No More Faking Fine* and *Your New Name*

"Most Christians find it difficult to offer original prayers. Even the disciples asked Jesus to teach them to pray. In *Crowned in Promise*, Kimberly Willingham Hubbard shows how to pray some of the most important prayers of all—for our children. It is a fresh and needed resource for all parents."

—CAL THOMAS, syndicated columnist

"As mother to two dear little girls, I know life as a parent is BUSY. In the hectic rush of keeping our kids fed, clothed and well-loved, we must prioritize covering our children in prayer. Wonderful tools like this prayer book, *Crowned in Promise* help us profoundly in this great endeavor!"

—REBECCA ST. JAMES, Christian artist and author

"I'm honored to recommend *Crowned in Promise* by Kimberly Willingham Hubbard. This will be one of the most valuable resources you'll find as you endeavor to raise your children in the nurture and admonition of the Lord. There is nothing more powerful or effective in loving your kids to maturity than God's Word and prayer. Reading and praying these one hundred promises from God over your children—and continuing to do so once they are adults—will enrich your family life and draw you all to intimacy with the Father. Perhaps even more important, it will raise them up in the imperative practice of habitual and ceaseless prayer."

—DAVID LIMBAUGH is a lawyer, a nationally syndicated columnist, and *New York Times* best-selling author of *Jesus is Risen*

Crowned in Promise

100 Prayers for Your Children

Kimberly Willingham Hubbard

FIDELIS
BOOKS

A FIDELIS BOOKS BOOK
An Imprint of Post Hill Press

Crowned in Promise:
100 Prayers for Your Children
© 2020 by Kimberly Willingham Hubbard
All Rights Reserved

ISBN: 978-1-64293-382-6
ISBN (eBook): 978-1-64293-383-3

Cover design by Cody Corcoran
Interior design and composition, Greg Johnson, Textbook Perfect

No part of this book may be reproduced, stored in a retrieval system,
or transmitted by any means without the written permission of the
author and publisher.

Unless otherwise indicated all Scripture is from THE HOLY BIBLE,
NEW INTERNATIONAL VERSION®, NIV® Copyright © 1973, 1978,
1984, 2011 by Biblica, Inc.® Used by permission.

Post Hill Press
New York • Nashville
posthillpress.com

Published in the United States of America

To my precious children, Joel and Winnie

May you grow in wisdom, stature, and in favor
with God and man. I pray you marvel at the works
of our Creator's hands and run full force into the
cloud of blessings he has spoken over your lives.
I love you, sweet warriors. Embrace God's abundant
grace and never let go.

"Be not ye afraid of them: remember the Lord,
which is great and terrible, and fight for your brethren,
your sons, and your daughters, your wives,
and your houses."
Nehemiah 4:14 (KJV)

Contents

A Parent's Call to Prayer

Children are a heritage from the Lord,
offspring a reward from him. Like arrows in the
hands of a warrior are children born in one's youth.
Blessed is the man whose quiver is full of them.

PSALM 127: 3-5 (NIV)

As parents, we have a high and mighty calling to raise children who will impact the next generation. Praise be to God he has bestowed upon us this beautiful blessing! However, along with the precious gift of children comes the weighty responsibility of imparting to our little ones the truths of God. This responsibility should not be taken lightly.

We live in a society that elevates "self-righteousness" over God's righteousness. Our culture is crumbling before our very eyes. We are inundated with media telling us to live contradictory to what Scripture states. Our children are deemed "worthy" and "popular" by the number of social media followers they have and not by the virtue of their character.

Our society is backward because "the whole world lies in the power of the evil one" (1 John 5:19 ESV). Nevertheless, it is confusing the hearts and minds of our kids. That is why it is imperative, as Christian parents, we communicate effectively to our children what is right and what is wrong even if it's unpopular. We must lead through example and take an active role in shaping their lives—so they will be able to discern what is of the world and therefore terminal and what is truly lasting in the Kingdom of God.

Sadly, we cannot single-handedly change the direction our society is headed and ultimately our children will be faced with many daunting decisions in life. Yet, we can individually empower our children to shine brightly for Jesus in the midst of the darkness; so, when they are faced with these difficult choices and crossroads in their lives, our children will be solidly established in the promises of Christ.

This empowerment begins in the home through a powerful, scripturally rooted prayer life.

There is an urgency today to teach the future generation the importance of calling to God not just in the middle of their struggles (as a lifeline) but in the everyday. There is also an urgency for children's parents to powerfully claim the promises of God over their children's lives.

It is time to start exercising the practice of prayer because prayer unleashes God's power!

God's Word tells us, "For all the promises of God in Him are Yes, and in Him Amen, to the glory of God through us" (2 Corinthians 1:20). However, if we fail to claim these promises, we miss out on this richness mindfully interwoven throughout the Bible.

We have been given a powerful tool from our Heavenly Father—a direct channel to his heart through prayer. Every single time we call out through spoken voice, quiet thoughts or even groans, our God Almighty hears us. Scripture tells us he hears the prayers of the righteous (Proverbs 15:39).

Please use these prayers in the following pages as a guide in your journey to pray over your children, born or unborn, and to teach them about prayer. Each specific, themed prayer is laced with God's powerful promises. You may want to substitute your child's or children's names for the generic terms in italics used in the prayers or read them as they are if you're not sure yet who's in your womb.

Let's begin crowning our children with God's promises and using Scripture to speak the truths of Christ's power and provision over our kids' lives.

This way we can successfully train them up in the habit of prayer, teach them God's Word, and display to them Christian leadership through a godly, steadfast example.

Section One

Power and Protection

This world is not our own. In fact, Scripture tells us, "For our struggle is not against flesh and blood, but against the rulers, against the authorities, against the powers of this dark world and against the spiritual forces of evil in the heavenly realms" (Ephesians 6:12). However, we have a Heavenly Father who has overcome this world. Every power of evil trembles at the mention of his name (James 2:19). It is vitally important our children are aware of the principalities at war for their precious hearts and minds. This is a serious battle and it should be treated as such.

As the Israelites smeared blood over the doorframes of their houses in the days of Moses, it's critical we claim God's promises of security and might over our children, families, and homes. Praise be to God, he has equipped us with mighty truths to conquer fear, stand up to the darkness, and suit up with his impenetrable battle armor.

Recite these prayers of power and protection over your little ones. Beseech God to cover your children in his feathers and under his secure wings (Psalm 91:4). May these promises encourage your children to stand unafraid of the arrows by night and walk confidently as mighty warriors of the King of Kings.

1

Safety

The name of the LORD is a fortified tower;
the righteous run to it and are safe.

PROVERBS 18:10 (NIV)

Power and Protection

Dear Lord,

You are the secure tower. We place our trust in you alone, God. You hide us in the shadow of your wings (Psalm 17:8) and cover us from harm in the cleft of your mighty mountain (Psalm 27:5). May we always seek refuge in you.

I pray you will wrap your wings of protection and safety around *my child*. In a world that grows darker by the day, defend and envelop *my little one* in your safe covering. Place your angels around *his/her* bedside (Psalm 91:11). Wherever *his/her* feet take *him/her*, I pray your safety encircles *him/her* like a wide-reaching net. You alone, Lord, make us dwell in safety (Psalm 4:8).

I claim this beautiful promise of protection in your sweet name, Jesus. Thank you for keeping my *little one* safe and secure. Illuminate the path in front of *my child's* feet. May *my son/ daughter* walk unscathed and march forward bravely with your purpose and power.

In Jesus's Name, Amen.

2

Bravery

You are my hiding place; You preserve me from trouble; You surround me with songs of deliverance.

PSALM 32:7 (NASB)

Power and Protection

Heavenly Father,

You have commanded us to be strong and courageous! May we step out with this lionlike bravery every single day. Instill your valiant courage into *my son/daughter's* character. Like Joshua, I pray *he/she* truly takes to heart your promises assuring us you will go before us in every battle we face (Deuteronomy 31:8).

May *my sweet child* hold fast to the truth that *he/she* will be victorious through you because you have already won the battle (John 16:33). I pray *my little one* clings to your words and steps out boldly in faith knowing *he/she* is guided and safeguarded by the Rock of Ages (Isaiah 26:4).

Build up courage like a raging fire in *my child's* soul. I pray *my little one* wears your bravery as a badge on *his/her* chest. May *my little one* roar confidently like a mighty, fierce lion—for you have given *him/her* the strength to conquer giants in your name (1 Samuel 17:45)!

In Jesus's Name, Amen.

3

Strength

*But those who hope in the LORD will renew their
strength. They will soar on wings like eagles;
they will run and not grow weary;
they will walk and not be faint.*

ISAIAH 40:31 (NIV)

Power and Protection

Dear Lord,

You are great and abundant in strength, God (Psalm 147:5). May my *son/daughter* depend on your strength and might, sweet Savior. You tell us you are our refuge and strength, an ever-present help in trouble (Psalm 46:1).

I pray your overwhelming power will be evident in *my child's* life. May *my little one* carry your strength with *him/her* and use it as *his/her* prized shield (Psalm 28:7). May *he/she* truly run and not grow weary and walk and not faint because *he/she* is fueled by your might and your might alone.

In *my son/daughter's* weakness—you are strong (2 Corinthians 12:9-10). May *my child* never forget that vital promise. *He/she* is in your hands, Lord. Uphold *my little one* and enable *him/her* to confidently tread on the highest of heights (Habakkuk 3:19).

In Jesus's Name, Amen.

4

Confidence

*This is the confidence we have in approaching God:
that if we ask anything, according to his will,
he hears us.*

1 JOHN 5:14 (NIV)

Righteous Father,

You have bestowed such love and mercy on us—while we were still sinners, you died for us, God (Romans 5:8). Grant my *son/daughter* the confidence to approach your throne of grace unashamed (Hebrews 4:16)! Being made new in you we can now draw near to you with freedom and confidence (Ephesians 3:12).

I pray *my child* gains confidence in your presence and *he/she* desires to present all *his/her* dreams, petitions, problems, cares, and worries to you! May you be *my child's* confidence and keep *his/her* foot from being caught (Proverbs 3:26).

Thank you, Father, for clearly showing *my child* the perfect path to take. I pray *he/she* will boldly seek your will in all *he/she* does. May *my little one* look to the heavens and the stars you know by name and state, "Great is our Lord and mighty in power; his understanding has no limit" (Psalm 147:5).

In Jesus's Name, Amen.

5

Security

*Jesus Christ is the same yesterday and today
and forever.*

HEBREWS 13:8 (NIV)

Power and Protection

Dear Lord,

In you we are fortified. You have promised us that no weapon formed against us will prosper (Isaiah 54:17). We rest assured in that glorious promise. I truly pray *my child* will feel your security today and always.

May *my little one* desire to plant *his/her* feet on the bedrock of your faithful promises (Psalm 40:2). I pray *he/she* will truly seek after the security you give (Psalm 9:10). May my *son/daughter* claim the truth in your Word that notes, "The name of the Lord is a strong tower; the righteous run into it and are safe" (Proverbs 18:10).

May *my little one* rest in the security of your everlasting nature and ever-present power. Fashion and form *him/her* into a mighty mountain—one that stands fixed in violent storms. Thank you for stabilizing *his/her* feet and vowing that *he/she* will not be shaken (Psalm 16:18)!

In Jesus's Name, Amen.

6

Power

Behold, I give unto you power to tread on serpents and scorpions, and over all the power of the enemy: and nothing shall by any means hurt you.

LUKE 10:19 (KJV)

Mighty God,

It is you who made the earth by your power, who established the world by your wisdom, and by your understanding stretched out the heavens (Jeremiah 10:12). We praise you for you are abundant in power and your understanding is beyond measure (Psalm 147:4-5).

I pray *my son/daughter* is clothed with power from on high (Luke 24:49) and *he/she* will forever proclaim your power to this new generation and your mighty miracles to all who come after *him/her* (Psalm 71:18).

May *my child* feel your great presence in *his/her* midst and know you as a victorious warrior who rejoices over *him/her* with shouts of joy (Zephaniah 3:17). It is written that you, the God of Israel, give strength and power unto your people (Psalm 68:35). May *my son/daughter* receive this gift of power with open arms.

In Jesus's Name, Amen.

7

Fearlessness

Though an army encamp against me,
my heart shall not fear; though war arise against me,
yet I will be confident.

PSALM 27:3 (ESV)

Power and Protection

Wonderful Counselor,

Your Word tells us that with your help we can advance against a troop; with you, God, we can scale a wall (Psalm 18:29). May this type of godly fearlessness dwell in the heart of my child. I pray *he/she* knows nothing is impossible for you (Luke 1:37).

You are the one who goes before us. I thank you, Father God, for fighting on *my child's* behalf (Deuteronomy 1:30). May *my son/daughter* trust and not be afraid and say boldly in the face of fear—the Lord God is my strength and song, and He has become my salvation (Isaiah 12:2).

Walk beside *my child* and lead the way, Lord. May *he/she* suit up with your armor and charge into the battle of life unafraid for you are the Lord God who has promised to fight for *him/her* (Joshua 23:10)!

In Jesus's Name, Amen.

8

Surefooted

He makes me as surefooted as a deer,
enabling me to stand on mountain heights.

PSALM 18:33 (NLT)

Power and Protection

God,

You are our firm foundation. In you our feeble feet are stabilized. You have commanded us to build our house on the solid rock of your nature (Matthew 7:25). I pray *my child* chooses to construct *his/her* house on your solid foundation.

May *my child's* feet stand securely fixed on the bedrock of your promises for there is no Rock like our Rock (Deuteronomy 32:31). I pray your law is in *my child's* heart so none of *his/her* steps shall slide (Psalm 37:31). You have promised you will not allow our feet to slip. I praise you for you are *my child's* protector and you do not slumber (Psalm 121:3).

Guide *my little one* in your truths and may *he/she* never veer off the path you have laid out before *him/her*. Thank you, God, for making *his/her* feet like the feet of a deer and enabling *him/her* to tread skillfully on the heights (Habakkuk 3:19).

In Jesus's Name, Amen.

9

Carefulness

Be careful what you say and protect your life.
A careless talker destroys himself.

PROVERBS 13:3 (GNB)

Father,

You have warned us that the days are evil. I pray *my child* is careful in the steps *he/she* takes and *he/she* is wise, making the best use of *his/her* time fully understanding your will (Ephesians 5:15-17). Sin so easily entangles; I pray *my son/daughter* will break free of any harmful binding chains and truly fix *his/her* eyes on you—the author and perfecter of our faith (Hebrews 12:1).

May *my little one* only desire to walk on the illuminated path of your grace and mercy. Your Word has commanded us to guard our steps when we go to the house of God. I pray *my son/daughter* will draw near to listen to you speak rather than uttering useless words (Ecclesiastes 5:1). I pray *his/her* heart is guarded—for everything *he/she* does flows from it (Proverbs 4:23).

Cultivate a cautious character in *my child's* life so *he/she* may examine everything set before *his/her* eyes and test whether it is of you. Your Word tells us everything good comes from you. Every perfect gift is from you alone (James 1:17). May *he/she* recognize this beautiful gift.

In Jesus's Name, Amen.

10
Boldness

The wicked flee when no one is pursuing them,
but the righteous are as bold as a lion.

PROVERBS 28:1 (CSB)

Power and Protection

Lord,

You are the mighty lion from the tribe of Judah and the root of David (Revelation 5:5). May *my child* latch on to your boldness and never let go. I pray *he/she* exhibits courage in the face of fear and holds out your sword of the spirit (Ephesians 6:17) bravely into the darkness.

Build up and train *my child* to be a good soldier marching for you—never entangling *himself/herself* in civilian affairs. May *my child* desire to please you—for you are the commanding officer (2 Timothy 2:3-4).

Thank you, God, for creating a heart of valor in *my little one*. May *he/she* fully comprehend it is you who arms *him/her* with strength for battle (Psalm 18:39). When you speak, all adversaries flee. Thank you for showing your unfailing love to your anointed (Psalm 18:50). Please continue to send down showers of blessings over *my child's* life (Ezekiel 34:26).

In Jesus's Name, Amen.

11

Deliverance

You are my hiding place; You preserve me from trouble;
You surround me with songs of deliverance.

Psalm 32:7 (NASB)

Power and Protection

Blessed Redeemer,

We collectively cry out, "Greater is he who is in me, than he who is in this world" (1 John 4:4). Thank you for delivering us from the dark grasp of death. You have liberated us from ultimate demise! May *my child* fully comprehend that you will deliver *him/her* from every obstacle in this life.

I pray *my little one* confidently walks like the Israelites through the parted Red Sea. You promise every step your children take are protected (Psalm 121:8). May *my son/daughter* sing, "I sought the Lord, and he answered me and delivered me from all my fears" (Psalm 34:4).

You are the God who sends out your word and heals. Thank you for delivering *my son/daughter* from destruction (Psalm 107:20). Rescue *him/her* from the things this world will throw *his/her* way. I pray you will give *my little one* the supernatural power to stand securely in faith and speak truth to the lies being spewed.

In Jesus's Name, Amen.

12

Persistence

Stand firm, and you will win life.

LUKE 21:19 (NIV)

Gracious Father,

You have told us to not grow weary of doing good, for in due season we will reap, if we do not give up (Galatians 6:9). Make *my child* a runner—one who does not tire chasing after you.

Line *his/her* feet with good news (Isaiah 52:7). You, the God who does not slumber, has promised that our feet will never slip (Psalm 121:3). Secure *my child's* steps on *his/her* journey—sprinting after your everlasting treasures.

You have said endurance produces character, and character produces hope (Romans 5:3-4). May *my child's* character shine like the moon in the night sky. Breathe into *his/her* life the endurance needed to finish *his/her* course. May *my little one* shout at the finish line, "I have fought a good fight, I have finished my course, I have kept the faith" (2 Timothy 4:7).

In Jesus's Name, Amen.

13

Zealous

Never be lacking in zeal, but keep your spiritual fervor,
serving the Lord.

ROMANS 12:11 (NIV)

God,

You have called us your very own and we burn for you with a zealous fire. May *my child's* desire for this passion consume *his/her* life. I pray *he/she* is never lacking in zeal, keeping your spiritual fervor in *his/her* heart always (Romans 12:11).

May *my son/daughter* proclaim, "I have been very zealous for the Lord God Almighty" (1 Kings 19:10) as Elijah did so very long ago. May your joy burn intensely in *his/her*—so passionately it is evident to all, *he/she* serves a great God and King (Psalm 95:3)!

I pray *my child* wraps your zeal around *himself/herself* as a cloak (Isaiah 59:17) and *he/she* wears this garment honorably. Your word says it is good to be zealous providing the purpose is moral (Galatians 4:18). May this pure and holy zeal for your house consume *my child's* life (Psalm 69:9).

In Jesus's Name, Amen.

14

Alert

*This is why it is said: "Wake up, sleeper,
rise from the dead, and Christ will shine on you."*

EPHESIANS 5:14 (NIV)

Father,

We praise you for you are the God who never sleeps nor slumbers. You are guardian for your people, and you promise you will watch over us and shelter us in your presence (Psalms 121:4-5). As you are alert God, I pray *my little one* is spiritually watchful in this wearisome world.

You have said, "My Presence will go with you, and I will give you rest" (Exodus 33:14). I pray *my little one* experiences this rest in you; however, sleeps with the sword of the spirit within *his/her* grasp. You have called your children to stand ready for battle. Prepare *my child's* hands for battle so *his/her* arms can bend a bow of bronze (Psalm 18:34).

Your word instructs us to stay awake at all times (Luke 21:36). May *my child's* eyes be fixed on the goodness of your promises. Thank you, God, for instructing, teaching, and counseling with your eyes upon *my child* (Psalm 32:8). Fine tune *his/her* steps to be in sync with your ways. I pray, even in sleep, *he/she* focuses on your perfect kingdom.

In Jesus's Name, Amen.

15

Attentive

*Be sober-minded; be watchful. Your adversary
the devil prowls around like a roaring lion,
seeking someone to devour.*

1 Peter 5:8 (ESV)

Mighty Maker,

Your word says, "Blessed is the man who listens to me, watching daily at my gates, waiting at my doorposts" (Proverbs 8:33-34). I pray our hearts are always sensitive to the leading of your Holy Spirit.

May *my child* stay sober-minded and alert with perseverance (Ephesians 6:18). Make *his/her* eyes, ears, and mind attentive to the things of you and are not of you. I pray your word, God, is a lamp to *my child's* feet and a light to *his/her* path (Psalm 119:105).

May *my little one* remain cautious—waiting, watching, and staying awake for you and your glory so *he/she* might be blessed (Revelation 16:15).

In Jesus's Name, Amen.

16

Health

Is anyone among you sick? Let them call the elders of the church to pray over them and anoint them with oil in the name of the Lord. And the prayer offered in faith will make the sick person well; the Lord will raise them up. If they have sinned, they will be forgiven.

JAMES 5:14-15 (NIV)

Jehovah Raffa,

You are the great physician. You are the beautiful healer. You have said by your wounds, Lord, we are healed (Isaiah 53:4-5). In your hands you offer complete healing. With one breath you can bring healing to our bodies.

You have proclaimed, "I am the Lord who heals you" (Exodus 15:26)! I believe that truth and trust your words when you say you will restore health and heal our wounds (Jeremiah 30:17). While you walked this earth as a man, you performed healing miracles; and you continue to perform great and mighty miracles even to this day!

I petition you to breathe health and wellness over *my child's* life. Not only in *his/her* physical life but also in *his/her* spiritual life. May *my child's* bones and body stay strong and may *his/her* desire for your words remain principal to *his/her* life—for you satisfy more than the richest of foods (Psalm 63:5).

In Jesus's Name, Amen.

17

Courageous

*Be strong and courageous, for you shall give this
people possession of the land which I swore to their
fathers to give them.*

JOSHUA 1:6 (NASB)

Power and Protection

Warrior King,

You have charged us to be strong and courageous. You have said do not be afraid or discouraged, for you are with us (1 Chronicles 28:20). We claim this promise of courage over our lives and thank you that the victory rests with you (Proverbs 21:31).

I pray *my little one* marches forward in confidence with you by *his/her* side. Please make *him/her* bold with strength in *his/her* soul (Psalm 138:3). May you gird *my precious child* with strength for battle (Psalm 18:39) and give *him/her* a true victory mindset.

As you shut the lions' mouths so they would not hurt Daniel (Daniel 6:22), I praise you for closing any avenues of evil that would harm *my child*. May *my child* truly take to heart what you have commanded to never be afraid but simply—believe (Mark 5:36).

In Jesus's Name, Amen.

Section Two

Godly Character

The Lord longs for his children to walk in his holiness. In his word, he has given us instructions to follow so we can live blameless and righteous lives. As Children of the Living God, we should aspire to reflect Godly characteristics in our lives. By our good fruit we should be known to others (Matthew 7:20).

Thankfully, God knows we are human and ultimately are broken vessels. He shows us repeatedly in Scripture that he uses ordinary people to do extraordinary things. We do not have to be perfect to radiate his light. Our missteps should not paralyze us; but, powerfully push us to pursue his righteousness (Psalm 21:21).

It is critical to pray Godly character traits over your children. It's important to familiarize their minds with what Scripture says is noble and pure. The world will flamboyantly push its agenda on our little ones; so, they must be outfitted with the knowledge of God's Truth. Claiming powerful promises of Godly character over our children's lives routinely will help them distinguish between what is true and what is counterfeit.

18

Honesty

*Therefore, each of you must put off falsehood and
speak truthfully to your neighbor, for we are all
members of one body.*

EPHESIANS 4:25 (NIV)

Godly Character

Dear Jesus,

You take delight in people who are trustworthy (Proverbs 12:22). Line *my little one's* lips with truth. May *he/she* only aspire to speak honestly and openly—even if it's not the popular thing to do.

I pray *he/she* strays far away from deceitful speech (1 Peter 3:10), and God, whatever is true, whatever is noble, whatever is right, whatever is pure, whatever is lovely, whatever is admirable—if anything is excellent or praiseworthy—that *he/she* will think and talk about such things (Philippians 4:8-9).

May *my child* desire to please you with *his/her* mouth and raise *his/her* voice with honest cries—articulating the greatness of *his/her* Maker! I pray *he/she* is a megaphone of your unfailing love, mercy, and constant love (Isaiah 63:7).

In Jesus's Name, Amen.

19
Gentleness

Let your gentle spirit be known to all men.
The Lord is near.

PHILIPPIANS 4:5 (NASB)

Godly Character

Dear Father,

You are strong and courageous; yet, you are also meek and gentle (2 Corinthians 10:1). You have listed gentleness as a fruit of the spirit (Galatians 5:22-23) and have charged us to have a spirit of gentleness (Galatians 6:1).

Your words instruct us to speak evil of no one, to avoid quarreling, to be gentle, and to show perfect courtesy toward all people (Titus 3:2).

I pray *my son/daughter* will have a strong yet gentle heart. May *he/she* seek goals with a firm desire but also remember to love others and to do to others as *he/she* would have them do to *him/her* (Luke 6:31).

In a world that values coarse, callous talk, I pray *his/her* words are truly polite, uplifting, and tactful. May *my child's* speech stir away any forms of wrath and may *his/her* lips truly speak wisdom. (Proverbs 15:1-7).

In Jesus's Name, Amen.

20

Respect

Show proper respect to everyone,
love the family of believers,
fear God, honor the emperor.

1 Peter 2:17 (NIV)

Godly Character

Jesus,

We respect and revere you. You are have set the perfect example for us to follow. Like you washed your disciples' feet, we are to wash the feet of others (John 13:14). Build up *my child's* character. May *he/she* mirror righteousness and show respect to others. May courteous words easily flow from *his/her* lips (Proverbs 16:24).

I pray *he/she* desires to honor *his/her* mother and father (Ephesians 6:1-3) for this is a commandment with a beautiful promise. I pray that *he/she* will truly be devoted in love to those around *him/her* and honor others above *himself/herself* (Romans 12:10).

May *he/she* respect all people, love the brotherhood, fear you, God, and show the proper respect to those placed in positions of authority over *him/her* (1 Peter 2:17).

In Jesus's Name, Amen.

21
Self-Control

*No temptation has overtaken you except what is
common to mankind. And God is faithful;
he will not let you be tempted beyond what you can
bear. But when you are tempted, he will also provide a
way out so that you can endure it.*

1 CORINTHIANS 10:13 (NIV)

Godly Character

King of Kings,

Keep *my little one* away from temptation. May *he/she* learn the art of self-control at an early age. May *his/her* flesh temple act as a fortified wall (Proverbs 25:28) protecting *his/her* heart from evil.

This world is so backward, calling good "evil" and evil "good" and the devil parades as an angel of light. May *my child* be able to differentiate between what is counterfeit and what is real (1 John 4:1).

I pray you will truly guard *his/her* heart (Proverbs 4:23) and *his/her* mind. May *his/her* feet turn from every form of wickedness.

I pray *he/she* desires to walk away from anything that would not be pleasing to you, Lord. Since you have called us to live by the Spirit, may *my child* keep in step with your Holy Spirit (Galatians 5:25).

In Jesus's Name, Amen.

22

Integrity

The integrity of the upright guides them,
but the unfaithful are destroyed by their duplicity.

PROVERBS 11:3 (NIV)

Godly Character

Wonderful Counselor,

You have promised the upright will inhabit the land and those with integrity will remain in it (Proverbs 2:20-21). May *my son/ daughter* walk in integrity today and always.

May *he/she* desire to seek out this truth. I pray it will spring out of *his/her* life like a bubbling brook (Proverbs 18:4). Oh Jesus, may *my child* desire to live honorably in every way (Hebrews 13:18).

When faced with tough decisions beyond *his/her* control, I pray *he/she* walks in the way of you, Lord (Deuteronomy 5:33). Lace *my child's* shoes with your integrity.

Mold and shape *my child* into a *man/woman* of character. May this character not just be an attribute but truly woven into the fibers of *his/her* existence!

In Jesus's Name, Amen.

23

Genuine

I will not set before my eyes anything that is worthless.
I hate the work of those who fall away;
it shall not cling to me.

Psalm 101:3 (ESV)

Maker,

We praise you for you are sincere. Your word ensures us that those who are proven to be genuine will receive the crown of life you promised to those who love you (James 1:12). We take you at your word because they are trustworthy and true (Revelation 22:6).

Please build up an authentic nature in *my child*. May *he/ she* model *his/her* life after you—the God who is alive, true, and genuine (1 Thessalonians 1:9). I pray *my child's* faith is also genuine (1 Peter 1:7) and *his/her* character is one that draws others toward the brilliant light of your majesty.

May *my child* surround *himself/herself* with authentic friends—ones who yearn to reflect your character and goodness to others. Your word tells us the righteous choose their friends carefully (Proverbs 12:26). Place your hand on *my child* and allow *him/her* to be drawn only to those who exhibit an honest nature.

In Jesus's Name, Amen.

24

Hardworking

*The soul of the sluggard craves and gets nothing,
while the soul of the diligent is richly supplied.*

PROVERBS 13:4 (ESV)

Godly Character

God,

Since the beginning of creation, you have called your children to work (Genesis 2:15). You entrusted your children with your handiwork and have promised the desires of the diligent are fully satisfied (Proverbs 13:4).

Create within *my child's* spirit a hardworking disposition. I pray *he/she* does not desire to chase worthless things but labors to reap a harvest with plenty of bread to provide for *his/her* family (Proverbs 12:11). May *my son/daughter* fully comprehend that all hard work brings a profit, but mere talk leads only to poverty (Proverbs 14:23).

I pray your favor, Mighty God, rests on *my child* and you will establish the work of *his/her* hands (Psalm 90:17). May *my son/daughter's* hands be diligent, committing to you whatever *he/she* does, for you have promised you will establish *his/her* plans (Proverbs 16:3).

In Jesus's Name, Amen.

25

Righteousness

The path of the righteous is level; you, the Upright One,
make the way of the righteous smooth.

ISAIAH 26:7 (NIV)

Godly Character

Lord,

You make the path of the righteous smooth. Your word tells us ill-gotten treasures have no lasting value, but righteousness delivers from death (Proverbs 10:2). I pray *my little one* chases after what is of eternal worth.

May *my child* tightly clutch *his/her* breastplate of righteousness (Ephesians 6:14) and march forward in this world dressed in your full armor. You have said the one who sows in righteousness, reaps a sure reward (Proverbs 11:8). May *my child* sow in righteousness, God!

I pray *my son/daughter* steadfastly desires the rewards of heaven and hungers and thirsts after your righteousness (Matthew 5:6) for it is your justice that rolls on like a river and your righteousness that is like a never-failing stream (Amos 5:24)! May *my child's* walk be blameless that *he/she* may be given fine linen, bright and clean, to wear (Revelation 19:8).

In Jesus's Name, Amen.

26

Slow to Anger

*In your anger do not sin: Do not let the sun go down
while you are still angry, and do not give
the devil a foothold.*

EPHESIANS 4:26-27 (NIV)

Godly Character

Lord,

You have said anger does not produce the type of righteousness you desire. I pray, God, that *my sweet child* is truly quick to listen, slow to respond, and slow to become angry (James 1:19, 20). Giving in to worry or anger will only lead to trouble (Psalm 37:8).

God, please rid *my child's* spirit of any type of anger, rage, malice, slander, and filthy language (Colossians 3:8). Paint your harmony over *him/her*. May *my son/daughter* act in a respectable manner that pleases your heart.

Breathe your calmness into *my child's* heart. May *he/she* prove *himself/herself* to be wise, calm, and collected. May *my child* never be overcome by foolish wrath (Proverbs 29:11). Fill *him/her* with your peace—so *he/she* may reap a harvest of righteousness (James 3:18).

In Jesus's Name, Amen.

27

Peace

Let the peace of Christ rule in your hearts,
since as members of one body you were called to peace.
And be thankful.

COLOSSIANS 3:15 (NIV)

Godly Character

Dear Lord,

You are the one who brings peace to our troubled hearts. Your word tells us you will grant peace in the land—we will lie down and no one will make us afraid (Leviticus 26:6).

I pray for the peace that passes all understanding to encircle *my child's* life (Philippians 4:7). You have promised us this covenant of peace—and have said it will not be removed (Isaiah 54:10). I praise you for that beautiful vow!

May this peace truly serve as a ruler over *my son/daughter's* heart and mind. I pray *he/she* seeks after peace and that *he/she* will truly pursue it with every fiber of *his/her* being (1 Peter 3:11). You say those who promote peace have joy (Proverbs 12:20). Give *my child* the joy only your peace can usher in!

In Jesus's Name, Amen.

28

Responsibility

If you are faithful in little things, you will be faithful in large ones. But if you are dishonest in little things, you won't be honest with greater responsibilities.

LUKE 16:10 (NLT)

Godly Character

Sweet Jesus,

In your word, it says each one of us will give an account of ourselves to you (Romans 14:12). Root *my child's life* in responsibility. I pray *he/she* takes on this important mantle of duty and steps up to the challenge of being a godly, accountable *man/woman*.

God, as *my child* grows in you, may immature talk flee from *his/her* mouth and may all *his/her* infantile ways dissolve (1 Corinthians 13:11). Your word says train up a child in the way *he/she* should go and when *he/she* is old, *he/she* will not depart from it (Proverbs 22:6).

I pray *my child* will always cling tightly to your truths and find value in your promises. Fashion *my child* into a responsible person and one day a *husband/wife* and *father/mother*. May *his/her* foundation in you always stick with *him/her* (1 Corinthians 3:14)!

In Jesus's Name, Amen.

29

Leadership

Before I formed you in the womb, I knew you,
before you were born, I set you apart;
I appointed you as a prophet to the nations.

Jeremiah 1:5 (NIV)

Godly Character

Sweet Savior,

Develop *my child* into a *man/woman* of loyal leadership. You have set *him/her* apart for a great and mighty purpose and have appointed *him/her* to lead others to your kingdom and preach the word (2 Timothy 4:2). May *he/she* be completely cleansed from what is dishonorable so *he/she* will be a vessel for honorable use—set apart as holy (2 Timothy 2:21).

Mighty King, I pray the leadership *my child* possesses is one of strength and dependence on you. May *he/she* have the attitude of humility because when humbleness is sought after you will lift *him/her* up (James 4:10).

I pray *he/she* truly stands out as an example for believers in speech, in conduct, in love, in faith, and in purity (1 Timothy 4:12) and flourishes like a tree planted by streams of living water (Jeremiah 17:8).

In Jesus's Name, Amen.

30

Virtue

Create in me a clean heart, O God;
and renew a right spirit within me.

PSALM 51:10 (KJV)

Beautiful One

You adore those who are pure in heart (Matthew 5:8) and those who offer their bodies as a living sacrifice, holy and pleasing to you (Romans 12:1). May *my son/daughter* strive to live as a virtuous *man/woman* in this scandalous society.

Lord, I pray *my little one* runs away from temptations of the flesh, and truly values what your words have said, are pleasing in your sight. You delight in uprightness (1 Chronicles 29:17) and have petitioned us to live in moral excellence (2 Peter 1:5).

May *my child* put to death whatever belongs to *his/her* earthly nature: sexual immorality, impurity, lust, evil desires, and greed, which is idolatry (Colossians 3:5) and live a life, holy and acceptable unto you!

In Jesus's Name, Amen.

31

Discernment

Beloved, do not believe every spirit, but test the spirits to see whether they are from God, for many false prophets have gone out into the world.

1 JOHN 4:1 (ESV)

Godly Character

Sweet Jesus,

You tell us to test the spirits on this earth because there are many false prophets who masquerade as fruitful benefactors (1 John 4:1). May we not be fooled by these wolves in sheep's clothing (Matthew 7:15).

Sharpen *my child's* mind to discern what is your good, pleasing, and perfect will (Romans 12:2). May *he/she* truly acquire wisdom and ask for the wisdom only you can offer *him/her* (1 Kings 3:9).

I pray *he/she* values wisdom and truly fastens this precious gift tightly around *his/her* neck (Proverbs 6:21). May *my child* never be deceived by the evil that parades itself as light in this dark world. I pray *my child* has the strength to say "get behind me" to every sinful practice and person that crosses *his/her* path (Matthew 16:23).

In Jesus's Name, Amen.

32
Gratefulness

Give thanks in all circumstances;
for this is the will of God in Christ Jesus for you.

1 THESSALONIANS 5:18 (ESV)

Godly Character

Redeemer,

You have called us to give thanks in all circumstances (1 Thessalonians 5:18)—in the good and in the bad. Let only praise flow from the lips of *my son/daughter*! You are still a mighty God in the midst of troubles. You assure us that when we pass through the waters, you will be with us (Isaiah 43:1-2).

When situations seem bleak, I pray *my child* learns to recount all your wonderful deeds (Psalm 9:1) and praise you in the storm—seeking out the promise after the rain. May *my little one* know you are always good and your sweet mercy endures forever!

May *my child* look to the heavens and the earth and praise you—for all of your creation is good (1 Timothy 4:4). I pray *he/she* serves you with gladness and comes into your presence with thanksgiving in *his/her* heart (Psalm 100:1-2).

In Jesus's Name, Amen.

33

Outgoing

But sanctify the Lord God in your hearts:
and [be] ready always to [give] an answer to every man
that asketh you a reason of the hope that is in you
with meekness and fear.

1 Peter 3:15 (KJV)

Godly Character

Heavenly Father,

May *my child's* heart swell with excitement. Bless him/her with an outgoing nature. May *my son/daughter* live *his/her* life with the pure delight of those welcoming you on the donkey with palm branches shouting, "Hosanna in the highest" (Mark 11:9-10)!

Your word tells us, "Let the one who boasts, boast in the Lord (2 Corinthians 10:17). I pray any bragging *my child* does in this life will be about you, God. May *he/she* gregariously tell others about your never-ending mercy and unfathomable grace for while we were still sinners you died for us (Romans 5:8).

Grant *my child* your great joy and may the sound of *his/her* rejoicing be heard from afar (Nehemiah 12:43). I pray *my son/ daughter* will be quick to proclaim your saving acts in the great assembly. May *my child's* lips never be sealed from telling of your restorative and matchless help (Psalm 39:9-10).

In Jesus's Name, Amen.

34

Charismatic

*Those who have insight will shine brightly
like the brightness of the expanse of heaven,
and those who lead the many to righteousness,
like the stars forever and ever.*

DANIEL 12:3 (NASB)

Godly Character

Marvelous Maker,

You have summoned us to be filled with the spirit (Ephesians 5:18). May all who encounter *my child* truly experience your captivating charisma in *his/her* life. I pray my *son/daughter* worships you in spirit and truth (John 4:24).

Thank you for preparing a lavish banquet for your people—a feast of rich food (Isaiah 25:6). May *my child* desire to sit at the table you have prepared for *him/her* and may *his/her* cup overflow! (Psalm 23:5).

Like a mirror, I pray *my child* joyfully reflects you, God. I pray *his/her* personality draws others to your throne room of grace. Like Moses' face shone brightly after conversing with you on the mountaintop, I pray *my child's* countenance gleams with your pure light because *he/she* keeps in constant contact with you (Exodus 34:29-35).

In Jesus's Name, Amen.

35

Patient

Whoever is patient has great understanding,
but one who is quick-tempered displays folly.

PROVERBS 14:29 (NIV)

Godly Character

God,

Your word has advised us not to be quickly provoked for anger resides in the lap of fools (Ecclesiastes 7:9). Often you desire your children wait patiently for your beautiful blessings. May *my child* learn there is beauty in the waiting and pristine character is developed in the darkroom.

I pray *my little one* waits patiently for you to magnificently move. Thank you for the powerful promise that you will turn to *him/her* and hear *his/her* cries (Psalm 40:1). May *my child* learn patience in *his/her* youth (Lamentations 3:25-27).

Thank you for longing to be gracious to us, Lord. Your word has gloriously promised, "Blessed are all who wait for you" (Isaiah 30:18)! May *my child* obtain this blessing while *he/she* waits for your abundance. I pray *he/she* will exhibit unwearied understanding—for you are never slow in keeping your promises (2 Peter 3:9).

In Jesus's Name, Amen.

36

Upright

Light is sown like seed for the righteous
and gladness for the upright in heart.

PSALM 97:11 (NASB)

Godly Character

Faithful Father,

Your word promises that even in darkness light dawns for the upright (Psalm 112:4). May *my little one's* character exude the bright light of an honorable nature. Create in my child a clean heart and renew a steadfast spirit within *him/her* (Psalm 51:10).

With every breath *my child* takes, breathe your integrity into *his/her* life. I pray it is evident *he/she* walks in the light as you are in the light (1 John 1:7). May *my child* truly shine like bright lights in a world full of crooked and perverse people (Philippians 2:5).

I pray *my child* desires to walk uprightly—for you have promised no good thing will you withhold from those who walk uprightly (Psalm 84:11). May *my little one* look to the heavens and know you are ordering *his/her* steps.

In Jesus's Name, Amen.

37

Optimistic

And we know that for those who love God all things
work together for good, for those who are called
according to his purpose.

ROMANS 8:28 (ESV)

Maker,

You have called your children to be joyful servants. Your word tells us you will never leave or forsake us (Hebrews 13:5). We praise you for this amazing promise—for even though we walk through the darkest valley, we will fear no evil, for you are with us (Psalm 23:4).

May *my child* observe life through optimistic lenses. I pray *he/she* will be filled with your spirit—addressing others with psalms and hymns and spiritual songs—singing and making melody to you and you alone with all *his/her* heart (Ephesians 5:18).

You have never forsaken those who seek you (Psalm 9:10). May *my little one* carry this joy and promise as *he/she* navigates through this life. I pray *my child* rejoices always (1 Thessalonians 5:16) for he knows you hold *his/her* life in palm of your mighty hands.

In Jesus's Name, Amen.

38

Wisdom

If any of you lacks wisdom, you should ask God,
who gives generously to all without finding fault,
and it will be given to you.

James 1:5 (NIV)

Godly Character

Dear God,

Your word says it is much better to get wisdom than gold, to choose understanding rather than silver (Proverbs 16:16). I beseech you on behalf of *my child* for that wisdom! May your insight and guidance encircle *him/her.*

Please shower your solid, ironclad wisdom over my *son/ daughter's* life. I pray *he/she* seeks out your knowledge and understanding—for it is more precious than sparkling, treasured gems (Proverbs 3:13-14). I truly petition you to breathe your wisdom into *my child's* thoughts and actions.

Like vines cling to fences, I pray *he/she* clings to the heavenly wisdom you impart for it is pure, peace-loving, considerate, submissive, full of mercy and good fruit, impartial, and sincere (James 3:17). In you alone are hidden all the treasures of wisdom and knowledge (Colossians 2:2-3). May *my child* reach out for the rubies of your truth!

In Jesus's Name, Amen.

Favored, Chosen, and Loved

We are loved with an everlasting love. This love cannot be snuffed out because it has proven itself even in death on a cross. We are regarded in Scripture as heirs of God's glory (Romans 8:17). In Christ we are never insignificant or worthless. We are treasured and adored.

The weight of God's favor and provision should be emphasized to our children on a daily basis. Our little one's should know they are precious gems in the hand of God. In a culture where value is placed on temporal achievement, worldly fame, and instant gratification, it is critical to pray promises of heavenly success and Godly vision over our children. It's also vital our children know God cherishes their lives because they are his beautiful workmanship designed from the womb to uniquely shine.

Claiming promises that speak of everlasting crowns and heavenly rewards will place in our children's minds what truly is important—the cross of Christ and the Kingdom he is preparing. By declaring these blessings of God's favor and love over your children, they will absorb the wonderful truth that they are truly the apple of God's eyes—dearly loved, and forever prized.

39

Calling

*I pray that the eyes of your heart may be enlightened
in order that you may know the hope
to which he has called you, the riches
of his glorious inheritance in his holy people.*

EPHESIANS 1:18 (NIV)

Favored, Chosen, and Loved

Dear God,

You call your sheep by name and lead them out into pastures of provision (John 10:3). I pray we hear your voice and respond to your call. May *my sweet child* answer the calling you have breathed over *his/her* life.

I pray *he/she* listens for your instruction and fervently embraces your battle cry by fearlessly stating, "Here I am send me!" (Isaiah 6:8). May *my child* walk in a manner worthy of the calling spoken over *his/her* life (Ephesians 4:1).

Equip *him/her* to fight the battle before *him/her*—for many are called but few are chosen (Matthew 22:14). Thank you, Lord, for choosing *my sweet little one* to serve as a warrior in your army. May *he/she* stand strong, securely clothed in your full armor.

In Jesus's Name, Amen.

40

Productivity

Bless all his skills, LORD, and be pleased with the work
of his hands. Strike down those who rise against him,
his foes till they rise no more.

DEUTERONOMY 33:11 (NIV)

Favored, Chosen, and Loved

Sweet Savior,

You have called us to live productive lives. In fact, you charged us in the beginning to "be fruitful and multiply and fill the earth" (Genesis 1:28). May your favor, Lord God, rest on *my child.*

Establish the work of *my little one's* hands (Psalm 90:17). Open the floodgates of heaven and rain down your provision over *his/her* life. May *my child* look to the sky and clearly see you are the one showering great and many blessings over *his/her* life.

Jesus, I pray *my little one* diligently works here on this earth for your kingdom. May *he/she* truly give *himself/herself* over fully to your work. You have promised this labor will never be in vain (1 Corinthians 15:58). I pray *my little warrior* stands firm and becomes like a tree planted by streams of water—yielding fruit, remaining healthy, and prosperous (Psalm 1:3).

In Jesus's Name, Amen.

41

Success

Keep this Book of the Law always on your lips;
meditate on it day and night, so that you may be
careful to do everything written in it.
Then you will be prosperous and successful.

Joshua 1:8 (NIV)

Favored, Chosen, and Loved

Jehovah-Jireh,

Your word promises that if we delight ourselves in you, you will give us the desires of our heart (Psalm 37:4). Thank you for opening your hand and satisfying the desire of every living thing (Psalm 145:16).

May *my little one* strive to truly savor your perfect goodness and the glory found in your nail scarred hands. I pray *my little one* acknowledges that apart from you, *he/she* has no good thing (Psalm 16:2). Like Joseph of old, may others see you are with my child and have granted *him/her* success in everything *he/she* does (Genesis 39:3).

Let your favor rest over *my child*, Lord. I pray you will establish the work of *his/her* hands that *he/she* might be successful (Psalm 90:17). Please open the windows of heaven for *my child* and pour down your beautiful blessing until there is no more need (Malachi 3:10).

In Jesus's Name, Amen.

42

Blessing

But blessed is the one who trusts in the LORD,
whose confidence is in him.

JEREMIAH 17:7 (NIV)

Favored, Chosen, and Loved

Sweet Savior,

You are the greatest blessing this world has ever encountered. I pray *my little one* will know the blessing of your redemptive grace. May *my son/daughter* cry out to you, "I beseech thee, send now prosperity," (Psalm 118:25), knowing full well true success comes from you.

May *my little one* look to you with high hopes and undiluted trust—for your word promises no good thing will you withhold from those whose walk is blameless (Psalm 84: 11). Give *my son/ daughter* a burning desire to walk on a virtuous, honorable path.

Your word says, "blessings crown the head of the righteous" (Proverbs 10:6). I pray *my child's* head is adorned with everlasting jewels from your Kingdom. Bless and keep *my child*. May your face shine upon *him/her*. Thank you, Lord, for being gracious to *my little one* and turning your face toward *my son/ daughter* (Numbers 6:24).

In Jesus's Name, Amen.

43

Vision

And afterward, I will pour out my Spirit on all people.
Your sons and daughters will prophesy, your old men
will dream dreams, your young men will see visions.
Even on my servants, both men and women,
I will pour out my Spirit in those days.

JOEL 2:28-29 (NIV)

Favored, Chosen, and Loved

Dear Lord,

We long for your perfect vision—for your ways and thoughts are higher than ours (Isaiah 55:9). May *my child* seek your vision, pursue your righteousness, keep your commandments, and write these promises down on the tablet of *his/her* heart (Proverbs 7:3).

I pray *he/she* has eyes to see you clearly (Matthew 13:16) and they are wide awake to witness the wonderful work of your hands. May *he/she* block out any frightening, discouraging talk from the powers of darkness—for the thief comes to steal and destroy; but you Lord have come to give a full and abundant life (John 10:10).

May *my child* reach out for the everlasting life you offer! I pray your vision becomes *his/her* guide and you truly pour out your spirit over *his/her* life (Acts 2:17).

In Jesus's Name, Amen.

44

Devotion

You shall love the LORD your God with all your heart
and with all your soul and with all your might.

Deuteronomy 6:5 (NASB)

Favored, Chosen, and Loved

Dear Lord Jesus,

You are the one who has blessed us with your might. You are a consuming fire (Hebrews 12:28). May *my child* give *his/her* life over as an offering to you showing you gratitude in all things.

I pray *my little one's* heart is wholly devoted to you and *he/she* will walk in your statutes and keep your commandments (1 Kings 8:61). May *he/she* truly become a *man/woman* devoted to prayer (Romans 12:12) keeping alert always with an attitude of thanksgiving (Colossians 4:2).

I pray *my child* proclaims loud and clear that you are *his/her* Lord and *he/she* has nothing else good in *him/her*—besides you (Psalm 16:12). May the incense of *my child's* committed spirit be a sweet in fragrance—pleasing to you!

In Jesus's Name, Amen.

45

Passion

*Then his disciples remembered this prophecy from the
Scriptures: "Passion for God's house will consume me."*

JOHN 2:17 (NLT)

Favored, Chosen, and Loved

Dear God,

May we have a passion for your supreme glory—for your to kingdom come, your will to be done on earth as it is in heaven (Matthew 6:10). Consume *my son/daughter's* life with a burning passion and great zeal for your house! May *my child* wrap *himself/ herself* in this fervor like a warm winter coat (Isaiah 59:17).

I pray against any type of earthly lusts that may tempt *my son/daughter.* May *he/she* loudly say "no" to the worldly passions that wage war over *his/her* heart. Please enable *him/her* to embrace a self-controlled, upright, and godly life in this present age (Titus 2:11-12).

I petition you, Abba Father, to fill *him/her* with a heavenly hunger. You say blessed are those who hunger and thirst for righteousness for they shall be satisfied (Matthew 5:6).

In Jesus's Name, Amen.

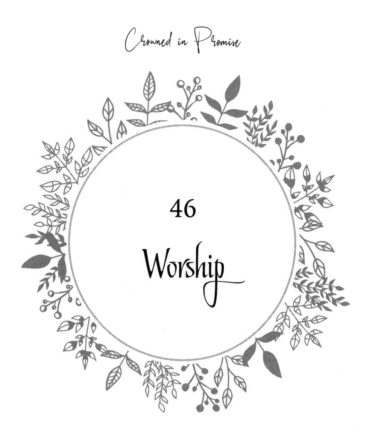

46

Worship

Ascribe to the LORD, you heavenly beings,
ascribe to the LORD glory and strength.
Ascribe to the LORD the glory due his name;
worship the LORD in the splendor of his holiness.

PSALM 29:1-2 (NIV)

Favored, Chosen, and Loved

Precious Lord,

You are great and do marvelous deeds; you alone are God (Psalm 86:10). This life is all about you, Jesus! May *my little one* sing to you a new song every single day (Psalm 96:1)! Place in the chambers of *my child's* heart a sweet melody—one that praises and uplifts your great name.

May *his/her* feet dance and jump at the mention of your greatness. I pray *my child* stands tall—and unashamedly makes a joyful noise unto you (Psalm 100:1). May *he/she* truly worship in spirit and in truth (John 4:24).

Oh, how beautiful to possess a heart of worship (Psalm 86:12). May worship be an essential part of *my son/daughter's* relationship with you!

In Jesus's Name, Amen.

47

Joy

*Though you have not seen him, you love him; and even
though you do not see him now, you believe in him
and are filled with an inexpressible and glorious joy,
for you are receiving the end result of your faith,
the salvation of your souls.*

1 Peter 1:8-9 (NIV)

Favored, Chosen, and Loved

Heavenly Father,

In you we find true, complete joy. We are filled with joy in your presence, God (Psalm 16:11). Grant *my sweet son/daughter*—pure, undiluted joy. I pray *my child* smiles ear to ear every day because *he/she* knows you love *him/her* and have great and mighty plans for *him/her* (Jeremiah 29:11).

May *his/her* heart overflow with sheer happiness at the thought of your great name (Romans 15:13). May *he/she* leap with joy over the realization you have given *him/her* a beautiful charge to proclaim your love to the nations (Mark 16:15)!

Jesus, work in *my child's* heart like only you can. May *his/her* life overflow with your inexpressible and glorious joy (1 Peter 1:9).

In Jesus's Name, Amen.

48

Affection

Love each other with genuine affection
and take delight in honoring each other.

ROMANS 12:10 (NLT)

Favored, Chosen, and Loved

King of Kings,

You display your great affection for us throughout the pages of Scripture. You have revealed to us what true love is—not that we loved you, but that you loved us and sent your Son as an atoning sacrifice for our sins (1 John 4:10).

You, my Lord, rejoice over us with singing (Zephaniah 3:17). I pray *my child* celebrates you in the same fashion and affectionately proclaims, "The Lord reigns, let the earth be glad; let the distant shores rejoice" (Psalm 97:1).

As the Apostle Paul did, may my child long for *his/her* brothers and sisters in Christ with your affection (Philippians 1:8). Additionally, may *his/her* mouth be open, and heart enlarged (2 Corinthians 6:11) to those who need to know of your loving-kindness. May the affection that only you can give flow out of *my child's* life.

In Jesus's Name, Amen.

49

Reverence

The Spirit of the Lord will rest on him—
the Spirit of wisdom and of understanding,
the Spirit of counsel and of might,
the Spirit of the knowledge and fear of the Lord
and he will delight in the fear of the Lord.

Isaiah 11:1-2 (NIV)

Favored, Chosen, and Loved

Mighty God,

We praise you because all dominion and awe belong to you! You establish peace in the heights (Job 25:2). I pray *my child* will look to you and affectionately shake at the mention of your name. May *my little one* view you as the King eternal, immortal, invisible, the only God of *his/her* heart (1 Timothy 1:17).

I pray *my child* serves you with a reverent fear and rejoices over you with trembling (Psalm 2:11). You are the God who parts the seas, opens the heavens, gives sight to the blind, and binds up the brokenhearted. Your kingdom cannot be shaken (Hebrews 12:28).

May *my little one* always honor and respect your commandments—for they breathe purpose and promise into *his/her* life. Your word tells us you give a banner to those who fear you (Psalm 60:4). May my child cling to this banner and praise you with awestruck wonder.

In Jesus's Name, Amen.

50

Refined

*My fruit is better than gold, better than even refined gold,
and my benefit surpasses the purest silver.*

PROVERBS 8:19 (ISV)

Favored, Chosen, and Loved

Lord,

Your voice is like the sound of raging waters. Your feet are like glowing bronze refined in a furnace (Revelation 1:5). You are the God of improvement and development. You long to see your children grow in you. May your word, Lord, refine *my child* (Psalm 66:12) and strengthen *his/her* walk with you.

I pray *my little one* desires to be you, gold refined in the fire that *he/she* may be rich (Revelation 3:18). When tested, may the genuineness of *my son/daughter's* faith be more valuable than gold (1 Peter 1:7). I pray *my child* will aspire to be a conduit of your truth.

Your word is very pure (tried and well refined). I pray *my child* loves your word with *his/her* whole heart (Psalm 119:140). May *he/she* learn to praise you through the refinement process—for you desire to make your children shine like the brightness of the heavens (Daniel 12:3).

In Jesus's Name, Amen.

51

Unwavering

Let us hold unswervingly to the hope we profess,
for he who promised is faithful.

Favored, Chosen, and Loved

Faithful Lord,

You are the God who never changes. Your love for us is unwavering and faithful. Though the storms of this life come, we know we will not be shaken because you are our fortress (Psalm 62:2). May *my child* declare all *his/her* days, "Praise God in heaven—for your love never fails" (Psalm 136:1). May *he/she* possess this kind of unwavering faith and love!

You have promised those who have remained steadfast are considered blessed (James 5:11). Grant *my child* this beautiful blessing. I pray *my son/daughter* truly draws near to your heart and seeks out your purpose in the cleft of your mighty mountain.

I pray *my little one* honors you aloud with *his/her* mouth and proclaims, "My heart is steadfast, O God, my heart is steadfast! I will sing and make melody" (Psalm 57:7). Mold and shape *my little one* to be a marble pillar in your temple bearing your holy name, God (Revelation 3:12).

In Jesus's Name, Amen.

52

Wonder

Many, LORD my God, are the wonders you have done,
the things you planned for us. None can compare with you;
were I to speak and tell of your deeds,
they would be too many to declare.

PSALM 40:5 (NIV)

Glorious Maker,

No one is like you God. You are majestic in holiness and awesome in glory. You work wonders (Exodus 15:11). You created beauty from nothing and hold this whole world in your mighty hands. I pray *my child* looks at this world you fashioned, in amazement.

May *he/she* find wonder in what seems simple to man—the vast ocean, rugged mountains, tranquil sunset, and cool breeze. They were all fashioned by your mighty hands and spoken words, Jesus. How glorious are the works of your hands (Psalm 19:1)!

May *my child* never cease to praise you for your spectacular nature. Oh Lord—I pray *my little one* stands in awe of your beauty every single day (Psalm 33: 8). May *my son/daughter* live in such a way that others are drawn to *his/her* amazement of your nature.

In Jesus's Name, Amen.

53

Love

*Dear friends, let us love one another, for love comes
from God. Everyone who loves has been born
of God and knows God. Whoever does not love,
does not know God, because God is love.*

1 John 4:7-8 (NIV)

Favored, Chosen, and Loved

Dear God,

You are the Father of love. We love because you first loved us, Sweet Savior (1 John 4:19). Let your love flow into *my son/daughter's* life. Surround *my child* with your shield of love (Psalm 5:12). I pray *he/she* has a burning passion, not only to love others, but a heart that loves and cherishes you, Lord.

May *my child's* heart be strong, yet also supple. Like King David of old, fashion *my son/daughter* to be a *man/woman* after your own heart (1 Samuel 13:14). May *he/she* experience love in this earthy life with *his/her* future spouse and iron-sharpening friends.

I pray *his/her* life is led by the deepest love of all—your blood, shed for *him/her* (Romans 5:8). We thank you for your true love that moved you to sacrifice all so we may have life!

In Jesus's Name, Amen.

Section Four

Living in Community

God has not called us to live in isolation. There is a network of believers on this earth God has intended us to work with for his heavenly purpose. As 1 Corinthians 12 explains, we are all one body with many members fashioned individually for a unique purpose. Nevertheless, when many personalities converge, it's easy to have misunderstandings and arguments. This type of behavior is not beneficial to the Kingdom of God. It stifles progress and clogs up the channels in which his children shine his light.

It is highly important to pray over your children's attributes that will help them live in community with other believers. In addition to this, it is also vital to pray over your little one's traits that will fill them with compassion and love toward unbelievers. After all, Christ came to seek and save all who are lost (Luke 19:10).

We need to encourage our children to build each other up in love (1 Thessalonians 5:11). Loving our neighbors as we love ourselves is a commandment in Scripture. May we claim these powerful promises of community over our children for two are truly better than one (Ecclesiastes 4:9).

54

Trustworthy

Show yourself in all respects to be a model of good
works, and in your teaching show integrity, dignity,
and sound speech that cannot be condemned,
so that an opponent may be put to shame,
having nothing evil to say about us.

TITUS 2:7-8 (ESV)

Living in Community

Lord,

You are trustworthy in all your promises and faithful in all you do (Psalm 145:13). We praise you because the works of your hands are truthful and just. All your precepts are sure, God (Psalm 111:7).

In all things may *my sweet child* show *himself/herself* to be a trustworthy *man/woman* of integrity. May *his/her* words reflect a dependable and true nature. May *he/she* love others deeply (1 Peter 4:8), wholly, and enthusiastically.

I pray *my child* proves to be a friend who can be counted on—a *man/woman* who will lend *his/her* coat to the cold, share *his/her* extra resources (Luke 3:11), and stop in *his/her* tracks like the Good Samaritan (Luke 10:33-37) to help those in dire situations.

In Jesus's Name, Amen.

55

Helpfulness

God is not unjust; he will not forget your work
and the love you have shown him as you have helped
his people and continue to help them.

HEBREWS 6:10 (NIV)

Miracle Maker,

We thank you for giving us the Holy Spirit as our helper. May we open our hearts to receive the instructions of your spirit at work in us (John 14:26). I pray you teach *my child* to hold up the hands of others—for this is a sacrifice pleasing to you (Hebrews 13:16).

You have given power to your children to do great and mighty things in your name. Like Aaron and Hur held up the hands of Moses (Exodus 17:12), impart to *my little one* the need to help others who are also walking in your ways.

True love is from you, God. Your word says everyone who loves is born of God and knows God (1 John 4:7). I pray *my child* will digest this truth and desire to assist others in their walk with you.

In Jesus's Name, Amen.

56

Thoughtful

The King will reply, "Truly I tell you,
whatever you did for one of the least of these
brothers and sisters of mine, you did for me."

MATTHEW 25:40 (NIV)

Precious Savior,

Develop a pure, steadfast heart within *my son/daughter* (Psalm 51:10). I pray *my child* adopts the servant hearted and considerate nature that comes only from you, Lord.

Your word tells us, blessed is he who considereth the poor: for you will deliver him in time of trouble (Psalm 41:1). May *my child's character* exude an overwhelming love and thoughtfulness to all your creation.

You are light and in you there is no darkness at all! I pray everywhere *my child* walks *he/she* will illuminate the dark places with your light (1 John 1:5). Develop in *him/her* an unselfish passion to serve others. I pray *he/she* always sees a masterpiece in the faces of others—formed by your hands!

In Jesus's Name, Amen.

57

Encouragement

Therefore encourage one another and build each other up, just as in fact you are doing.

1 Thessalonians 5:11 (NIV)

Beautiful Maker,

You are the God of signs and wonders. You always come through displaying your greatness like a firework display. We are at your right hand and you have promised us we will not be shaken (Psalm 16:8).

May *my son/daughter's* lips be filled with godly encouragement—the type that will spur others toward love and good deeds (Hebrews 10:24-25). I pray *my child* edifies others and others edify *him/her* as well. May this be one of *his/her* desires—to encourage and build up others daily (Hebrews 3:13).

You are the God who gives endurance and encouragement (Romans 15:5). Give *my child* a passion to inspire and cheer others on in their Christian walk and may *he/she* walk uprightly and value *his/her* fellow man on this earth.

In Jesus's Name, Amen.

58

Good Listener

He who gives an answer before he hears,
it is folly and shame to him.

PROVERBS 18:13 (NASB)

Awesome God,

You listen to our heartfelt petitions. Your ears are attentive to our prayers (1 Peter 3:12). May *my child's* ears be responsive to your precious instructions. You have said, "Blessed rather are those who hear the word of God and keep it" (Luke 11:28).

I praise you for listening to *my child's* voice, *his/her* pleas for mercy, and inclining your ear to *him/her* (Psalm 116:1-2). May *my son/daughter* be quick to hear, slow to speak, slow to anger, (James 1:19) for faith comes from hearing, and hearing through the word of Christ (Romans 10:17).

You have promised that everyone who hears your words and does them will be like a wise man who built his house on the rock (Matthew 7:24). I pray *my child* fervently listens to every word from your mouth—for it is the bread that provides *him/her* life!

In Jesus's Name, Amen.

59

Friendship

Walk with the wise and become wise,
for a companion of fools suffers harm.

PROVERBS 13:20 (NIV)

Precious Lord,

We praise you—for you are the friend who sticks closer than a brother (Proverbs 18:24). Surround *my son/daughter* with positive influences, Jesus. May kind, godly people be drawn to *him/her*; and may those who seek to harm and manipulate *him/her* be repelled quickly from *his/her* life (Deuteronomy 28:7).

It is written in your word, "He who walks with the wise grows wise, but a companion of fools suffers harm" (Proverbs 13:20). I pray *my son/daughter* finds iron-sharpening friendships (Proverbs 27:17). Please place in *my child's* life friends who are seeking you, desire to do your will, and live their fullest lives for you.

Above all, I pray *my little one* discovers true friendship with you—for you are the friend who sacrificed all on a cross of pure love (Philippians 2:8). May *my little one* desire to tell you the secrets in *his/heart* above all others.

In Jesus's Name, Amen.

60

Forgiving

Judge not, and you shall not be judged.
Condemn not, and you shall not be condemned.
Forgive, and you will be forgiven.

LUKE 6:37 (KJV)

Merciful Father,

You have forgiven our sins and saved our souls with your death on the cross. We can never repay you for this forgiveness. There is no one like you for you have compassion on us. You have trodden our sins underfoot and hurled all our iniquities into the depths of the sea (Micah 7:19).

I pray *my child* embraces your forgiveness with open arms. May *my son/daughter* confess *his/her* sins to you because you have promised you are faithful and just and will forgive and purify *him/her* from all unrighteousness (1 John 1:9).

May *my child* learn to exemplify kindness to others by forgiving them just as you have forgiven *him/her* (Ephesians 4:32). You have called us to forgive limitlessly (Matthew 18:22). Fashion *my child's* heart into one that demonstrates a compassionate character—for all have sinned and fallen short of the glory of God (Romans 3:23).

In Jesus's Name, Amen.

61

Collaborative

For the body is not one member, but many.

1 Corinthians 12:14 (NASB)

Living in Community

Father,

You have intended for the body of Christ to perfectly work together. I pray *my little one* learns to operate in a team with other believers. Your word tells us two are better than one, because they have a good reward for their toil; and, if one falls, the other will be there to lift the other up (Ecclesiastes 4:9-10).

I pray *my child* will exhibit a good attitude while he strives to work in a team with his brothers and sisters in Christ. Your word beautifully proclaims—how good and pleasant it is when brothers dwell in unity (Psalm 133:1)! May *my little one* seek out this unique unity and collaboration with other believers.

May *my child* truly be eager to maintain the unity of the Spirit in the bond of peace (Ephesians 4:3). I pray *he/she* will fully grasp the concept that in you—we are one body with many members—all with different functions (no one greater than the other). May *my son/daughter* recognize *his/her* purpose for the kingdom and use it for your glory!

In Jesus's Name, Amen.

62

Pleasant Talk

*Let no corrupting talk come out of your mouths,
but only such as is good for building up, as fits the occasion,
that it may give grace to those who hear.*

EPHESIANS 4:29 (ESV)

Savior,

Your Word says a gentle tongue is a tree of life (Proverbs 15:4). May *my child* embrace this beautiful blessing to sprout forth as an everlasting sapling. Season *my little one's* words with salt. May *his/her* communication always resonate pleasantly with grace (Colossians 4:6).

I pray *my child's* words will never be hasty (Proverbs 29:20) but always wisely weighed out in *his/her* mind. If anyone asks why *he/she* trusts in you, may *my little one's* answer be solid, reflecting gentleness and respect (1 Peter 3:15). I pray *he/she* truly desires to be like you, Lord.

May *his/her* speech always uplift and encourage others. I pray *my little one* will delight your heart, God, with *his/her* pleasant talk on this earth. Thank you for making *my child's* mouth that of the righteous—a fountain of life (Proverbs 10:11).

In Jesus's Name, Amen.

63

Intentional

Seek the Lord and his strength;
seek his presence continually!

1 CHRONICLES 16:11 (ESV)

Lord,

Your ways are deliberate. Your blessings are brilliantly thought-out. I pray *my child* lives *his/her* life with this sense of intentionality. May *my little one's* eyes look straight ahead, and *his/her* gaze be directly fixed before you. I pray *my child* gives careful thought to the paths of *his/her* feet that *he/she* will remain steadfast (Proverbs 4:25).

May *my child* examine sensibly how *he/she* walks, not as unwise but as wise. I pray *my little one* makes the best use of the time, because the days are evil (Ephesians 5:15-17). With every beat of *his/her* heart, may your purpose pump aggressively.

For such a time as this (Esther 4:14) you have placed *my child* upon this earth. I pray *his/her* life is one that makes a difference for your heavenly kingdom.

In Jesus's name, Amen.

64

Resourceful

And when they had eaten their fill, he told his disciples,
"Gather up the leftover fragments,
that nothing may be lost."

JOHN 6:12 (ESV)

Maker,

You are the God who provided mana and quail for the Israelites in the desert (Exodus 16). You are Jehovah-Jireh—our provider. I pray *my child* is responsible and resourceful with all you give *him/her*.

May *my child* never long for the frivolous fancies in this life—for these trivial delicacies fade; but, your blessings last forever. Your word tells us life is more than food and the body more than clothing (Luke 12:23). I pray *my child* carefully and wisely uses what you have provided for *him/her*.

You have promised that whoever can be trusted with very little can also be trusted with much and whoever is dishonest with very little will also be dishonest with much. (Luke 16:10). May *my child* prove *he/she* can be trusted with your everlasting abundance.

In Jesus's Name, Amen.

65

Hospitable

Above all, love each other deeply, because love covers over a multitude of sins. Offer hospitality to one another without grumbling.

1 PETER 4:8-9 (NIV)

Living in Community

Precious Lord,

You are the greatest example of hospitality this earth has ever seen. You welcome sinners to your table and invite them to share in your feast of plenty (Matthew 9:10). May *my child* follow your example and receive others into *his/her* life and home with your grace and love.

Shine your warmth and kindness through *my little one's* smile and actions. I pray *he/she* possesses the character of Lydia who welcomed Paul and Silas into her home after they were released from prison (Acts 16:40). May *my child* be an encouragement to others who are searching for your light of life.

I pray *my little one* lives by the phrase in your word, "When you enter a house, first say, 'Peace to this house'" (Luke 10:5). May my child carry your harmony with *him/her* wherever *he/she* travels. Bless the tracks of *his/her* feet. May *he/she* trample over hindrances with purpose and victory.

In Jesus's Name, Amen.

66

Peacemaker

*Mark the blameless and behold the upright, for there is
a future for the man of peace.*

PSALM 37:37 (ESV)

King of Kings,

You are the Prince of Peace and the Lord of Lords (Isaiah 9:6). We rest safely and securely in your hands. Pump your peace through *my child's* veins, Lord. I pray anxiety and worry will be absent from *his/her* life. I claim the powerful promise that mercy, peace, and love will be *my child's* in abundance (Jude 1:2).

May peace be within *my child's* walls and security within *his/her* towers (Psalm 122:6-7). I pray my son/daughter will never seek out chaos but will choose to eliminate this type of confusion—for it is not from you. May *my little one* illustrate to others your peace-loving wisdom, Father (James 3:17).

May an overwhelming passion to carry out your goodwill consume *my little one's* life. Your word tells us, "Blessed are the peacemakers, for they shall be called sons of God" (Matthew 5:9). I pray *my child* aspires to be called a peacemaker in this life.

In Jesus's Name, Amen.

67

Balance

*And Jesus increased in wisdom and in stature
and in favor with God and man.*

LUKE 2:52 (KJV)

Living in Community

Dear God,

Create balance in *my child's* life. You have given us a charge to minister to others on this earth and fulfill your will. I pray, Lord, that while *my child* races to *his/her* calling that *he/she* will operate in the world but not be of it (John 17:16).

May *my son/daughter* learn to live with others on this soil—laboring hard in diligence and devotion but with a heavenly mindset. You have told us—the harvest is plentiful but the workers are few (Matthew 9:36).

Oh God, I pray *he/she* seeks first your kingdom and your righteousness because you have told us all things will be added to us if we do this (Matthew 6:33)! May *my child* learn to live in favor with both you and man all while wholeheartedly consecrating *himself/herself* to you. I pray *he/she* desires you more than anything on earth (Psalm 73:5). 28.

In Jesus's Name, Amen.

68

Communication

Let your speech always be gracious,
seasoned with salt, so that you may know how
you ought to answer each person.

COLOSSIANS 4:6 (ESV)

Lord,

Scripture says—a word, fitly spoken, is like apples of gold in a setting of silver (Proverbs 25:11). May *my child's* communication shine forth to all like silver and gold.

I pray the words of *my child's* mouth and the meditations of *his/her* heart are pleasing to you (Psalm 19:14). May *my little one's* speech be active, effective, and gracious. Season *my child's* words with salt so *he/she* can articulate and communicate efficiently with others.

I pray *my son/daughter* is a faithful envoy who truly brings about healing in *his/her* speech (Proverbs 13:17). Consume *my child's* voice with your words, Father. I humbly ask, Lord Jesus, that others will not hear *him/her* speaking, but your Spirit speaking through *him/her* (Matthew 10:20).

In Jesus's Name, Amen.

69

Empathy

Rejoice with those who rejoice,
weep with those who weep.

ROMANS 12:15 (ESV)

Merciful Savior,

You have told us to bear one another's burdens (Galatians 6:2). We are all one body in you, Christ Jesus. If one part suffers, all the parts suffer with it (1 Corinthians 12:25-26). As you wept for the struggles, heartaches, and misfortunes of others on this earth, I pray a sense of this kind of empathy is established in *my son/daughter's* life (John 11:33-35).

While I pray *his/her* life is safeguarded from struggle and heartache, I pray *he/she* develops a passion to reach out to the hopeless and hurting. May *my child's* heart truly break over what breaks your heart, God (Romans 9:1-3).

I pray *my child* is the type of friend or stranger who cares enough to lend a helping hand, offer an attentive ear, or say a fervent prayer for those hurting and destitute. May *my child's* empathy and compassion for others always point to you.

In Jesus's Name, Amen.

70

Humility

Live in harmony with one another. Do not be proud
but be willing to associate with people of low position.
Do not be conceited.

PROVERBS 12:16 (NIV)

God,

You oppose the proud but give grace to the humble (James 4:6). Your word also states that with humility comes wisdom (Proverbs 11:12). May this modesty run through *my son/daughter's* veins.

I pray *my child* will truly humble *himself/herself* before you and as a result, your word has said you will lift *him/her* up for this beautiful, sacrificial action (James 4:10). You, Lord, are abundant in power. Your understanding is beyond measure (Psalm 147:4-5). May *my sweet child* recognize where *his/her* strength is birthed.

I pray *he/she* boasts only in *his/her* weakness and how *his/her* dependence on you makes *him/her* strong; so, your ever-encompassing power will rest on *him/her* (2 Corinthians 12:9).

In Jesus's Name, Amen.

71

Fair

He has told you, O man, what is good;
and what does the Lord require of you
but to do justice, and to love kindness,
and to walk humbly with your God?

MICAH 6:8 (ESV)

Lord,

You are a God who shows no partiality; however, your word says anyone who fears you and does what is right is acceptable to you (Acts 10:34-35). May *my child* desire to do what is right in your eyes.

I pray *my son/daughter* will be an imitator of you in all *he/she* does—never twisting justice or what is right (Job 8:3). Give *him/her* a burning longing to treat others fairly and serve you with righteousness. May *my child* never pervert justice (Leviticus 19:5). I pray *he/she* is never afraid to speak up and judge fairly in this life (Proverbs 31:9).

May *my child* beseech you to travel on the ancient paths and walk in your good way (Jeremiah 6:16). We praise you and thank you for guarding the paths of justice and watching over the way of your saints (Proverbs 2:6-9). Safeguard the upright trail of *my child*.

In Jesus's Name, Amen.

72

Compassion

As you know, we count as blessed those who have persevered. You have heard of Job's perseverance and have seen what the Lord finally brought about. The Lord is full of compassion and mercy.

James 5:11 (NIV)

Prince of Peace,

You, oh Lord, are a God of compassion. I pray *my son/daughter* acquires true compassion for your children and all your hands have made (Psalm 145:9) for you delight to show mercy (Micah 7:18). May *his/her* heart be broken over what breaks yours—the lost, alone, and those who do not yet know of your greatness and faithfulness (Matthew 9:35-38).

I pray *my child* is a light in the dark places—for you have called *him/her* to walk as a child of the light (Ephesians 5:8). May *my child* show concern for those who are down and out, riddled with sickness, and heavily loaded with despair.

May *he/she* be clothed with compassion, kindness, humility, gentleness, and patience (Colossians 3:12). Lead *my child* in the way *he/she* should go and remind *him/her* to dress every day in the uniform of compassion.

In Jesus's Name, Amen.

73

Loyalty

*He who pursues righteousness and loyalty finds life,
righteousness and honor.*

PROVERBS 23:23 (NASB)

Living in Community

Dear God,

We praise you because you keep your covenant with us! You are the faithful God (Deuteronomy 7:9). Your word tells us that even if we are unfaithful, you will remain faithful—for you cannot deny who you are—our loyal Savior! (2 Timothy 2:13).

May *my little one's* feet hold fast to your path. May *he/she* truly keep your way and not be turned aside (Job 23:11). We pray *my child* remains loyal and steadfastly anchored to your great name for all *his/her* days.

May *my child* mirror your faithfulness and loyalty through *his/her* actions and words to your children. We pray *he/she* holds fast the confession of *his/her* hope without wavering (Hebrews 10:23).

In Jesus's Name, Amen.

74

Servant Hearted

For even the Son of Man came not to be served
but to serve, and to give his life as a ransom for many.

MARK 10:45 (NIV)

Living in Community

Sweet Savior,

You said to your disciples, "If anyone wants to be first, he must be the very last, and the servant of all" (Mark 9:35). What a beautiful truth, God! May we seek to be servant hearted.

In a world that values self-aggrandizement, I pray *my child* fully comprehends that this life *he/she* has been given is not just about *him/her*. May *he/she* truly heed your words which tell us it is more blessed to give then to receive (Acts 20:35).

God, may *my child* desire to be an imitator of you (1 Corinthians 4:16) and embrace the freedom you have given us in you. I pray *he/she* uses this freedom to serve *his/her* fellow man humbly in love (Galatians 5:13). May *he/she* serve you and follow you all *his/her* days for you have said you will honor those who serve you (John 12:26).

In Jesus's Name, Amen.

75

Generosity

*Tell them to use their money to do good. They should
be rich in good works and generous to those in need,
always being ready to share with others.*

1 TIMOTHY 4:18 (NLT)

Father,

You are a generous Savior—for you have granted us redemption through your blood and have forgiven all our trespasses (Ephesians 1:7). May *my child's* heart pulse with generosity, graciousness, and compassion!

May *he/she* never harden *his/her* heart against those in need but give sufficiently (Deuteronomy 15:7-8) to those who are less fortunate and alone. Your word says a generous person will prosper; whoever refreshes others will be refreshed (Proverbs 11:25). I pray *he/she* desires to refresh the dry basins of the parched.

As *he/she* gives to others, I pray *my child's* spirit is also revitalized. Sweet Lord, thank you for placing your hands on *him/her* and calling *him/her* blessed in this land (Psalm 41:1-2).

In Jesus's Name, Amen.

76

Humorous

He will yet fill your mouth with laughter
and your lips with shouts of joy.

JOB 8:21 (NIV)

Maker,

Thank you for the gift of laughter. Your word tells us a cheerful heart is good medicine (Proverbs 17:22). I pray *my child's* personality will sparkle forth with pure bliss. May *my little one* develop a good sense of humor and an inextinguishable joy.

I pray *my child* will laugh without fear of the future because *he/she* knows who holds tomorrow in his hands (Proverbs 31:25). I pray *he/she* sits at the banquet table with you daily. Your Word promises for the happy heart, life is a continual feast (Proverbs 15:15).

May *my child's* mouth always be filled with laughter and *his/her* tongue with joyful songs—for you have done spectacular things for us (Psalm 126:2-3). I praise you for filling *my little one's* heart with gladness (Psalms 4:7).

In Jesus's Name, Amen.

Section Five

The Christian Walk

It should be our daily prayer to align our hearts with God's will. As Christians we are called to deny ourselves, take up our cross, and follow Christ (Luke 9:23). Our spiritual walk is a personal journey full of twists and turns—some joyous and some truly terrifying. We must equip ourselves with the proper tools needed to confront fear, live virtuously, and stand firm on God's precepts.

When we seek the Lord, he will answer us and deliver us from all our fears (Psalm 34:4). The key is being a willing vessel who cries out and desires to follow his illuminated footsteps. We must be ready to relinquish our old nature and chase after the qualities God so earnestly adores.

It is important our children witness a discipline and hunger coming from us, as parents, to walk in the light of Christ. These prayers, designed to speak blessing and fortitude over our children's individual relationship with God, will encourage them to walk confidently, serve willingly, and seek him steadfastly. May our children desire to lace up their tennis shoes, run the race set before them, and receive the spectacular eternal reward.

77

Innocence

Behold, I send you out as sheep in the midst of wolves;
so be shrewd as serpents and innocent as doves.

<small>MATTHEW 10:16 (NASB)</small>

The Christian Walk

Merciful Savior,

You were the innocent, spotless lamb slain for our sins. In a culture deteriorating day by day, may *my child* aspire to be holy as you are holy. I pray *he/she* longs to be someone whose spirit shows no deceit (Psalm 32:2).

May *my little one* pray as the psalmist did, "Keep back your servant from presumptuous sins; let them not have dominion over me" (Psalm 19:13). Shield *my son/daughter's* eyes from the things that would make *his/her* heart grow callous and numb.

May *my little one* long to retain childlike innocence—for you have said, "Let the little children come to me and do not hinder them, for to such belongs the kingdom of heaven" (Matthew 19:14. I pray *my child* will not share in the sins of others and will keep *himself/herself* pure (1 Timothy 5:22). You delight in innocence, Father. Your word tells us, "Blessed are the pure in heart, for they will see God" (Matthew 5:8).

In Jesus's Name, Amen.

78

Maturity

Brothers, do not be children in your thinking.
Be infants in evil, but in your thinking be mature.

1 CORINTHIANS 14:20 (ESV)

Sovereign Lord,

We have tasted and know you are indeed good! May *my little one* crave your true spiritual milk (1 Peter 2:2-3) so *he/she* will grow up established in your salvation. I pray *he/she* longs to truly move beyond elementary teachings and desires to dig deeper into the richness of your everlasting grace (Hebrews 6:1).

Develop within *my child* a character of maturity. Your word tells us we are to grow up in every way into him who is the head, into Christ (Ephesians 4:15). May *my little one* strive to place the mantle of your maturity over *his/her* life. I pray *he/she* flourishes like a flower in your sunlight.

May *my little one* learn to stand tall and strong like an age-old building. When the pressures of this world try to break down the exterior of my child, I pray *he/she* will persist with your power. Your word has promised the root of the righteous is immovable (Psalm 12:3). May *my son/daughter's* roots be fastened to the bedrock precepts of your truth.

In Jesus's Name, Amen.

79

Focus

For to be carnally minded is death;
but to be spiritually minded is life and peace.

<small>ROMANS 8:6 (KJV)</small>

Highest King,

May you always be the focal point of our lives. In you we live and move and have our being (Acts 17:28). Open *my child's* eyes. May *he/she* desire to be spiritually minded for *he/she* is a partaker of your heavenly calling. Fix *his/her* eyes on you (Hebrews 3:1).

Focus *my child's* attention on your honor, majestic splendor, and your amazing deeds (Psalm 145:5)! May *he/she* never grow distracted by short-lived beauty, vapid flattery, and surface conversations—for charm is deceptive and beauty is fleeting (Proverbs 31:30).

I pray *my child* dives deep into your mercy and bathes *himself/ herself* in your extensive, full-bodied grace. Oh Lord, may *he/she* fix *his/her* attention not on what is seen but on what is unseen; for what is seen is temporary but what is unseen is eternal (2 Corinthians 4:18).

In Jesus's Name, Amen.

80

Willingness

If you are willing and obedient,
you shall eat the good of the land.

ISAIAH 1:19 (NIV)

The Christian Walk

Sweet Savior,

You stand at the door of hearts and knock. I pray *my child* listens for your gentle knock and is willing to open the door to your goodness (Revelation 3:20) for you have promised you will come in and eat with *him/her*.

Please anoint *my child's* head with oil—so *his/her* cup overflows (Psalm 23:5). May *my little one* always offer you *his/her* first fruits willingly—for you have promised you will fill *his/her* barn with plenty when *he/she* does (Proverbs 3:9-10). I pray *he/she* acknowledges all blessings flow from your hands.

Upon hearing your voice say, "Whom shall I send? And who will go for us?" I pray *my son/daughter* will eagerly state, "Here am I. Send me!" (Isaiah 6:8). May *my child* desire to lace up *his/her* shoes and readily walk the path that leads others to your throne of grace.

In Jesus's Name, Amen.

81

Committed

And may your hearts be fully committed to the LORD
our God, to live by his decrees and obey his commands,
as at this time.

1 Kings 8:61 (NIV)

King of Kings,

You displayed the greatest act of loyalty and love by your death on the cross. I pray *my child* lives *his/her* life fully devoted to you, God. May *my little one* commit to you whatever *he/she* does—for you have promised you will establish *his/her* plans (Proverb 16:3).

Like a violent wave crashing into a shore, may your commitment wash over *my child's* character. I pray *he/she* embraces the blessed assurance of your beautiful salvation. I pray *my little one* draws near to you with a true heart in full assurance of *his/her* faith (Hebrews 10:22).

May *my child* devote *himself/herself* to the apostles' teaching and the fellowship of believers, to the breaking of bread, and the prayer (Acts 2:42). I pray *my little one* will never be ashamed of the gospel, for it is the power of God for salvation to everyone who believes (Romans 1:16).

Keep this Book of the Law always on your lips; meditate on it day and night, so you may be careful to do everything written in it. Then you will be prosperous and successful (Joshua 1:8).

In Jesus's Name, Amen.

82

Prayerfulness

Keep watching and praying that you may not enter
into temptation; the spirit is willing,
but the flesh is weak.

MATTHEW 26:41 (NASB)

God,

You have called your children to humble ourselves, pray, seek your face, and turn from our wicked ways with the beautiful promise that you will hear from heaven, forgive our sin, and heal our land (2 Chronicles 7:14). I pray *my child* truly longs to become a *man/woman* of prayer. May *he/she* devote *himself/ herself* to prayer–being watchful and thankful (Colossians 4:2).

As Daniel developed a practice of prayer and bowed on his knees before you (Daniel 6:10), I pray *my child* will one day yearn for this type of intimacy with you. You tell us we have not because we've asked not (James 4:2). May *my child* have the boldness to ask of you big things—for you are the God who rewards those who diligently seek you (Hebrews 11:6).

I pray *he/she* asks nothing out of selfish ambition or vain conceit (Philippians 2:3-4); but, *he/she* desires to see your kingdom come, your will be done, on earth as it is in heaven (Matthew 6:10).

In Jesus's Name, Amen.

83

Clarity

But you should keep a clear mind in every situation.
Don't be afraid of suffering for the Lord.
Work at telling others the Good News, and fully carry
out the ministry God has given you.

2 Timothy 4:5 (NLT)

The Christian Walk

Dear Lord,

You have called your people to have sound and renewed minds. I pray you will grant *my child* your clarity. May *he/she* see your path before *him/her* clearly and desire to develop the mind of Christ (1 Corinthians 2:16). Your word tells us you are not a God of confusion but of peace (1 Corinthians 14:33). May confusion flee from *my little one's* mind and your peace wash over *his/her* being.

May *he/she* recognize your perfect ways and yearn to follow you. Please shine in the heart of *my child* so *he/she* may know the light of the knowledge of the glory of God in the face of Jesus Christ (2 Corinthians 4:6). May the windows of *his/her* soul be translucent and absent of any type of grime that will stifle the pure light of you, God.

When others see *my child*, I pray they will clearly see you in *his/her* reflection. May *my little one* walk with an unveiled face (2 Corinthians 3:18) shining your Holy Spirit. You are the mighty King—the one who deserves all praise and acknowledgement.

In Jesus's Name, Amen.

84

Educated

Gold there is, and rubies in abundance,
but lips that speak knowledge are a rare jewel.

PROVERBS 20:15 (NIV)

The Christian Walk

Teacher,

You are recorded in Scripture as increasing in wisdom, stature, and in favor with God and man (Luke 2:40-52). I pray *my son/daughter* has a thirst for a godly education. May *he/she* willingly seek out your truths and yearn to apply these kernels of wisdom in *his/her* life.

I pray against any false teachers that desire to take *my child's* mind captive by philosophy and empty deceit, according to human tradition, according to the elemental spirits of the world (Colossians 2:8). May *my son/daughter* look to you alone for wisdom and cry out to you saying, "Teach me good judgment and knowledge, for I believe in your commandments" (Psalm 119:66).

Your word tells us, "An intelligent heart acquires knowledge, and the ear of the wise seeks knowledge" (Proverbs 18:15). May *my child* seek out an education firmly rooted in your good soil so *he/she* will hear your word and fully comprehend it (Matthew 13:23).

In Jesus's Name, Amen.

85

Observant

Heed instruction and be wise, and do not neglect it.
Blessed is the man who listens to me,
Watching daily at my gates,
Waiting at my doorposts.

PROVERBS 8:33-34 (NASB)

The Christian Walk

Lord,

You have charged your children to be sober in spirit and on the alert because our adversary, the devil, prowls around like a roaring lion, seeking someone to devour (1 Peter 5:8). I praise you—for you are the God who shows up in the darkness of lion's dens and miraculously closes the mouths of the blood thirsty wild beasts.

May *my little one* know you as the Warrior King who fights furiously for *his/her* heart. Your word promises you indeed contend with him who contends with us (Isaiah 49:25). Open my child's eyes wide so *he/she* may be able to decipher what is taking place around *him/her*. I pray *he/she* is spiritually and physically observant.

May *my son/daughter* pay close attention to what *he/she* has heard so *he/she* does not drift away from your truth (Hebrews 2:1). What an honor it is to be called your disciple! Grab hold of *my child's* soul. May *he/she* know the truth—for you have promised it will set us free. (John 8:31-32).

In Jesus's Name, Amen.

86

Dependence

I am the vine; you are the branches.
Whoever abides in me and I in him,
he it is that bears much fruit,
for apart from me you can do nothing.

John 15:5 (ESV)

Wonderful Maker,

Apart from you we can do nothing. Your spirit has made us and your breath has given us life—hallelujah (Job 33:4)! I pray *my little one* drinks from your everlasting water all *his/her* days and eats of your mana from heaven (John 6:50). May *my child* realize *his/her* deep need for you, Sweet Savior.

You tell us we cannot live by bread alone but by every word from your mouth (Matthew 4:4). May *my child* feast on your precious promises and rest in the assurance *he/she* is fully dependent upon your grace.

When asked who you are, I pray *my child* answers with utmost confidence, "He is the Christ, the Son of the living God" (Matthew 16:28).

In Jesus's Name, Amen.

87

Seeker

Those who know your name trust in you, for you,
LORD, have never forsaken those who seek you.

PSALM 9:10 (NIV)

The Christian Walk

God,

You truly draw near to those who seek you. We praise you for you are good to those whose hope is in you—the one who seeks you (Lamentations 3:25). May *my child* long to gaze into your face and chase after you every second of every day. You are worth pursuing. You are the eternal King!

I pray *my child* will look to you and your strength. I pray *he/she* will seek your face always (1 Chronicles 16:11). May *my little one* cry out like the psalmist King David, "You, God, are my God, earnestly I seek you; I thirst for you, my whole being longs for you, in a dry and parched land where there is no water" (Psalm 63:1).

May *my son/daughter's* hope be found in you, Lord. Encourage and refresh *my child's* soul as he/she eagerly chases after you on this earth. I pray *my little one* runs in such a way as to get the prize—an imperishable crown (1 Corinthians 9:24-25).

In Jesus's Name, Amen.

88

Faith

Now faith is confidence in what we hope for
and assurance about what we do not see.

HEBREWS 11:1 (NIV)

Covenant Keeper,

You have said if we have the faith of a mustard seed, we can move mountains (Matthew 17:20). May *my sweet child* develop a sincere faith—a bold, beautiful, zealous faith that does not waiver.

I pray *his/her* faith in you, Lord, is one that cannot be moved (Acts 2:25). May *his/her* feet be fixed on your promises that breathe life into all your children (Proverbs 3:26). In faith, I pray *my child* trusts you with *his/her* whole life and surrenders all *his/her* attention to seeking and knowing you fully. You are the air filling our lungs and giving us purpose!

Let *him/her* desire to walk in faith like the mighty, godly figures before *him/her* (Hebrews 11); and may *my son/daughter* be courageous enough to ask you to show *him/her* your radiant glory (Exodus 33:18)!

In Jesus's Name, Amen.

89

Creativity

*He has filled them with skill to do all kinds of work
as engravers, designers, embroiderers in blue, purple
and scarlet yarn and fine linen, and weavers—
all of them skilled workers and designers.*

EXODUS 35:35 (NIV)

The Christian Walk

Holy Lord,

You delight in creativity! In fact, you are the Master Artist who created the heavens and the earth (Genesis 1:1) and created mankind in your own image (Genesis 1:27). We praise you—for we are the clay and you are our potter; we are all the work of your hand (Isaiah 64:8).

I pray *my child* will be filled with your beautiful creativity and muse on the work of your hands (Psalm 143:5). May *he/she* desire to tap into the arts in order to celebrate your wonders.

May *my child* boldly hold up *his/her* banner (Psalm 20:5) and point to you with the marvelous works of *his/her* hands. You bestow talent upon your children. I pray *my son/daughter* embraces *his/her* talent and uses it to glorify you!

In Jesus's Name, Amen.

90

Fortitude

If the world hates you, know that it has hated me
before it hated you. If you were of the world, the world
would love you as its own; but because you are not of
the world, but I chose you out of the world,
therefore the world hates you.

JOHN 15:18-19 (ESV)

Dear Holy Father,

The Scripture tells us you were despised and rejected by mankind (Isaiah 53:3). It is hard to believe you, the beautiful Savior, were mocked and scorned by the very ones you came to save. We praise you for the sacrifice you made and the love you show each and every day to humankind.

This world is not our home. May *my child* cling to the truth which notes, here on earth we have no lasting city, but we seek the city to come (Hebrews 13:14). I pray *my son/daughter* will carry with *him/her* the spirit of fortitude on *his/her* Christian journey in this world. May *he/she* press forward with perseverance and powerfully repel the arrows of the enemy by day and night for your name's sake! Let not *his/her* heart grow weary (Revelation 2:3).

Create within *my child* a backbone of steel. We know in this world we will have troubles; but, you, precious Savior, have overcome the world (John 16:33). May *my child* march forward in this life with confidence and resolve—knowing it is you who weighs the motives of our hearts (Proverbs 16:2) not mortal man.

In Jesus's Name, Amen.

91

Energetic

*For this I toil, struggling with all his energy
that he powerfully works within me.*

COLOSSIANS 1:29 (ESV)

Powerful God,

We praise you—for your Word tells us the God of Israel gives power and strength to his people (Psalm 68:35). Grant *my child* abundant energy so *he/she* can stand tall and shine for you. May *my little one* be strengthened with all power according to your glorious might, God (Colossians 1:11).

I pray *my son/daughter* will never rely on what seems externally mighty, like chariots and horses, but *he/she* will trust in the name of the Lord our God (Psalm 20:7). May *my child* look to you only, Lord, to supply strength.

May your arm strengthen *my child* (Psalm 89:21). I pray *he/she* will refuel *his/her* body with your living water. Thank you for the beautiful promise that whoever drinks of your water (the Holy Spirit) shall never thirst (John 4:14). I pray *my child* desires to lap up your wellspring of energy and strength.

In Jesus's Name, Amen.

92

Understanding

Then he opened their minds
to understand the scriptures...

LUKE 24:45 (ESV)

Blessed Savior,

Your Scripture opens our hearts and minds to understand you more. May *my child* possess the knowledge of your Word and comprehend the great riches hidden in the promises on the pages of every Scripture verse *he/she* reads. May *my little one* trust in you with all *his/her* heart and lean not on *his/her* own understanding (Proverbs 3:5).

You tell us the unfolding of your Words gives light; it gives understanding to the simple (Psalm 119:130). May this light of understanding shine on *his/her* life. 1 pray *my child* receives your Word with great eagerness, examining the Scriptures daily (Acts 17:11) and you will truly open *his/her* mind to understand the Scriptures (Luke 24:45).

May your Holy Spirit work in *my child's* life teaching *him/her* all things and bringing to *his/her* remembrance all you have said (John 14:26). Thank you for showering over *my child* the precious gift of godly comprehension. May *my son/daughter* desire to bow daily to the Scripture which is God breathed (2 Timothy 3:16).

In Jesus's Name, Amen.

93

Intuition

For the word of God is living and active, sharper than any two-edged sword, piercing to the division of soul and of spirit, of joints and of marrow, and discerning the thoughts and intentions of the heart.

Hebrews 4:12 (NIV)

Rock of Ages,

May *my child* call out to you daily for your insight. I pray *he/she* will cry aloud for your understanding and truly search for it as for silver or a rare hidden treasure (Proverbs 2:3). I pray discretion will watch over *my child* and understanding will guard *his/her* life. Deliver *my son/daughter* from the way of evil (Proverbs 2: 11-12).

Gaining your intuition is essential as we walk this earth. May *he/she* truly test everything that is not of you and hold fast to what is good (1 Thessalonians 5:21).

I pray *my child* is able to discern between what is good and what is evil (Philippians 1: 9-10). May *he/she* walk in awareness of the forces of darkness battling against *his/her* spirit every second of the day.

In Jesus's Name, Amen.

94

Adventurous

"Come, follow me," Jesus said,
"and I will send you out to fish for people."

MATTHEW 4:19 (NIV)

The Christian Walk

God,

You called Peter to exercise great faith and walk upon the water. You commissioned the disciples to deny themselves, take up their cross and follow you (Matthew 16:24). Life with you, Lord, is an adventure because you often lead us into the great unknown.

I pray *my child* is willing to go where you send *him/her*. Like Abraham obeyed and went, without knowing where he was going, may *my child* possess this type of faith (Hebrews 11:8). May *my son/daughter* obey your voice—for you have promised you will be *my child's* God and *he/she* will walk in the way which you commanded, and it will be well with *him/her* (Jeremiah 7:23).

May *my child* replace feelings of fear with your peace that passes all understanding. For you have told us, "Do not be worried and upset; do not be afraid" (John 14:27). Develop an adventurous spirit within *my child* so *he/she* may run full force after your plan for *his/her* life.

In Jesus's Name, Amen.

95

Obedience

If you love me, keep my commands.

JOHN 14:15 (NIV)

The Christian Walk

Lord,

You have said, blessed are those who hear the word of God and obey it (Luke 11:28). May *my son/daughter* have the desire to walk in your commands and obey your instructions.

In your word, you have given us all we need to live a holy and upright life. I pray *my child* longs to follow your precepts so *he/she* will prosper in all *he/she* does and wherever *he/she* goes (1 Kings 2:3).

May *he/she* truly digest your commands, cherish them and take them to heart. I pray *he/she* delights in your law, Lord and meditates on it both day and night (Psalm 1:2). Give *my child* the endurance to obey in all circumstances. May *he/she* truly pick up *his/her* cross, deny *himself/herself* and follow you (Matthew 16:24).

In Jesus's Name, Amen.

96

Decisive

So, whether you eat or drink, or whatever you do,
do all to the glory of God.

1 CORINTHIANS 10:31 (NIV)

Prince of Peace,

You make known to us the path we should take. You say "Here is the road. Follow it" (Isaiah 30:21). May *my child* be able to recognize your voice and take the steps necessary to adhere to your commandments. My *he/she* truly seek not *his/her* own will but the will of you who sent him/her (John 5:30).

I pray *my child* will call to you for wisdom in decision making for you have promised you will answer *him/her* and tell *him/her* wonderful and marvelous things *he/she* knows nothing about (Jeremiah 33:3).

May *my child* not be like the wave of the sea driven with the wind and tossed; but may *he/she* follow the pattern of the sound words *he/she* hears from you (2 Timothy 1:13). I pray *my child* pursues you with unwavering faith—never doubting any promise written in your Word of Life.

In Jesus's Name, Amen.

97

Disciplined

My son, do not despise the LORD's discipline, and do not resent his rebuke, because the LORD disciplines those he loves, as a father the son he delights in.

– PROVERBS 3:11-12 (NIV)

Father,

It is written you discipline us for our good, in order that we may share in your holiness (Hebrews 12:10). I pray *my child* learns not to despise instruction. You have said those you love, you rebuke and discipline (Revelation 3:19). You do this so we may become more and more like you.

I praise you for blessing *him/her* with your discipline, Lord— for it is the way you teach from your law. Thank you for never rejecting your people and never forsaking your promised inheritance (Psalm 94:12-14). Great is your faithfulness (Lamentations 3:23).

I pray *my child's* heart is open to receive your vibrant instruction, God. Through your discipline, I pray *my child* will reap a harvest of righteousness and peace because *he/she* has been trained by it (Hebrews 12:11).

In Jesus's Name, Amen.

98

Motivated

Therefore, my dear brothers and sisters, stand firm.
Let nothing move you. Always give yourselves fully to
the work of the Lord, because you know
that your labor in the Lord is not in vain.

1 CORINTHIANS 15:58 (NIV)

The Christian Walk

Lord,

You have warned us to be careful not to practice our righteousness in front of others to be seen by them—for if we do, we will have no reward from you in heaven (Matthew 6:1). I pray the motivation of *my son/daughter's* heart is noble and sincere; so *my child* will obtain a beautiful eternal reward from you.

When *my child* prays and earnestly seeks you, I pray *he/she* goes into *his/her* room, closes the door and prays to you. You have promised this type of behavior will be rewarded (Matthew 6:5-6). I pray *my child* casts off anything that would satisfy *his/her* self-ambition and races toward what would please your heart.

May *my son/daughter* proclaim like you did, "My food is to do the will of him who sent me and to finish his work" (John 4:34). I pray *my child* boldly hold up *his/her* banner (Psalm 20:5) and point to you with the marvelous works of *his/her* hands.

In Jesus's Name, Amen.

99

Well-Grounded

For the time is coming when people will not endure sound teaching but having itching ears, they will accumulate for themselves, teachers to suit their own passions, and will turn away from listening to the truth and wander off into myths. As for you, always be sober-minded, endure suffering, do the work of an evangelist, fulfill your ministry.

2 Timothy 4: 5-6 (ESV)

The Christian Walk

Savior,

We collectively proclaim, "The Lord lives and blessed be my rock, and exalted be my God, the rock of my salvation" (2 Samuel 22:47). Fasten *my child's* feet to your unshakeable firm foundation. I pray you will serve as the support beams holding *my little one's* body together.

I praise you, Lord, for laying the foundation of the house of the Lord in *my child's* spirit (Ezra 3:11). May *he/she* truly grow up to be a well-grounded individual with roots growing deep into you and a life built on you (Colossians 2:7).

May *my child* truly desire to be a righteous root yielding much fruit (Proverbs 12:12). Like faithful Abraham, heir to your promise, I pray *my child* will look forward to the city with foundations, whose designer and builder is you. (Hebrews 11:10).

In Jesus's Name, Amen.

100

Availability

The LORD came and stood there, calling as at the other times, "Samuel! Samuel!" Then Samuel said, "Speak, for your servant is listening."

1 SAMUEL 3:10 (NIV)

The Christian Walk

Father God,

You are available to your children at every hour of the day. We thank you for not being an absent God. You are always by our side. Like you did for the Israelites in the wilderness, your presence hovers over us like the cloud by day and the pillar of fire by night (Exodus 13:21-22).

May *my child* never desire to hide from you like Adam and Eve in the garden of Eden. I pray *my son/daughter* will not feel ashamed in your presence but long to sup and commune with you—for you are a beautiful, loving, and loyal Creator. May *my little one* walk with you, like Enoch of the Old Testament (Genesis 5:24).

I pray *my son/daughter* will always be available to your call on *his/her* life. May *my child* be ready to walk the road you set before *him/her*. Your ways are always perfect, and your word is flawless (2 Samuel 22:31). Summon *my little one* to shine brightly for you. Unclutter *his/her* heart to be fully open to your guidance!

In Jesus's Name, Amen.

About the Author

Born and raised in Fort Worth, Texas, Kimberly Willingham Hubbard attended Baylor University and has worked for several news outlets. Kimberly, her husband, Taylor, and son, Joel, currently reside in Richmond, Virginia. She frequently blogs on her website: www.tradingpapercrowns.com.